NEED TO BE FREE

TRAPPED ALONE IN MY JOURNEY

NEED TO BE FREE

TRAPPED ALONE IN MY JOURNEY

CASSANDRA AVANCE

RoxxSteady Book Publishing

Michigan

Need to Be Free: Trapped Alone in My Journey

Copyright © 2014 by Cassandra Avance

RoxxSteady Book Publishing
Flint, Michigan
roxxsteadypublishing@gmail.com

All Scripture quotations, unless otherwise noted, are taken from the *Holy Bible: King James Version*®. KJV®. Copyright © 1976 by Thomas Nelson, Inc. All rights reserved.

All rights reserved.

No part of this book may be reproduced, scanned, or distributed in any printed or electronic form without permission. Please do not participate in or encourage piracy of copyrighted materials in violation of the author's rights. Purchase only authorized editions.

Paperback ISBN 978-0-692-91595-0

eBook ISBN 978-0-692-91596-7

To my husband, Quintin and children, Malachi, Matthew and Brooke. All of you are the reasons why I wake up every day, continue to live and thrive to be better. I love you.

CONTENTS

Dedication v

Introduction ix

Chapter 1 Help Me Now! 1

Chapter 2 I Once Was Young 9

Chapter 3 A Change is Gonna Come 19

Chapter 4 Uncommon Sense 29

Chapter 5 My Life Shattered 43

Chapter 6 Shambles…...59

Chapter 7 Engaged Again?…................................69

Chapter 8 Wedding Bells 81

Chapter 9 Marital Fits…Oops Bliss 87

Chapter 10 Divided Before the Fall 95

Chapter 11 Precious Delivery 119

Chapter 12 Weary and Wounded 133

Chapter 13 Something Brewing 149

Chapter 14 Moment of Truth 161

Chapter 15 Changing Hearts 169

Chapter 16 Readjustment 187

Chapter 17 One Last Time 205

Post-Logue Finally Free 219

Introduction

It has been impressed upon my heart to share my testimony. I know that I have gone through things to strengthen my faith, and my relationship with God. I have also had to experience things so that I can help someone else. It is through my experiences that I learned to serve the true and living God, not just the God that my parents served. I've learned to know Him for myself and have gained an intimacy with Him that I wouldn't have otherwise known. This story is an account of events that happened to me after I started walking in disobedience to God.

One thing that I've realized is, the enemy will take

your need to be loved and desire to feel validated and use it against you. Ignorance can become a trap. Sometimes you do things and only want to do it temporarily. The next thing you know, something temporary can change your life permanently. You can't go back in time and change the past. What you can do is learn from your experiences and use your knowledge for a greater purpose. Experience makes you wise. Wisdom is the key to living a purposeful and fulfilling life. "Wisdom is the principal thing; therefore get wisdom: and with all thy getting get understanding" Proverbs 4:7 KJV.

It is my prayer that through the experiences that I am about to share, someone will be delivered and set free. I want you to realize that you do not have to live your life through the pain of your past and that your past does not define your future. If you want change in your life, God can help you bring it to pass. I want young women to realize their self-worth and to not feel like they have to settle for anything just to be loved. Be blessed, be beautiful, and most importantly, BE FREE!

Chapter 1

Help Me Now!

Why is it that good people always get hurt? God I need You to help me now. I am getting tired of going through this alone. And I'm angry. I'm angry because the one person that was closest to me betrayed me. This has been the most painful experience of my entire life. This month, it will be three years that he's been gone out of our home, and almost two years that we've been divorced.

Knowing my ex-husband, Drew, brought me so much happiness in the beginning. And from the middle to the end, I experienced unspeakable amounts of pain; unspeakable because I don't think there are enough words in my vocabulary to adequately express how bad he hurt me. There have been things that have happened to me that over the years that I forced myself to forget because they were too painful to remember. He really hurt me to my core, I mean down to the center of my being. And at times I think I actually felt my heart stop beating. I didn't realize that I'd loved him so deeply, but I did. I gave him my heart, my body, my hand in marriage, three children (even though it was never in my plan to have any) and unfortunately my life. When he left me, a part of me died along with our marriage. It has been said that divorce is the closest thing to death and that once you go through something as traumatic as divorce, you'll never be the same mentally. I can attest to that. When our marriage died, it felt like he died, which essentially he did when he left God to live in sin. And I never thought that I would recover from it. Either he never knew, or he just didn't care that he was my best friend. He was everything that I wasn't. Where I was weak, he was strong. When I didn't know how to show love, he taught me. He was my balance. When he left, I lost my balance. If you know anything about balance, you can't walk or function without it. It has taken me this entire three years to get my balance back.

It had always seemed like Drew was the calm to my storm. He was always the voice of reason for me when I got hot-headed. Then, like a thief, he stole that calmness away and became a hurricane destroying everything in my life. The intense love that I'd once had for him transformed into anger and later, hatred. I hated him for pursuing me for all of those years just to break my heart and leave me stuck with three children while he was off living his life going from woman to woman and being a deadbeat dad. On top of defiling our marriage and committing adultery, he has become ruthless. He has no heart at all. The man I fell in love with cared about me and my feelings and would never disrespect me the way that he has.

I could see the change in him long before he left. I felt those other women in our bed while we were making love. The man I married respected my body; the person he'd become took advantage of it. There were times when he'd forget who he was in bed with. And each of those times cut like a knife and left a deep scar. I didn't realize until he'd started abusing me that I'd been abused all of my life. I'd been mentally and verbally abused. I've never been loved. Then he came along being the first person to really love me and I ended up being mentally, spiritually, physically and emotionally abused, and manipulated. I became afraid of him. I was afraid to disappoint him, afraid to hurt him, afraid of what he thought of me and of what he'd do if I didn't do what he wanted. Well, it turns out that I can think for myself. I can tell him no. I don't have to be afraid anymore. After all of this, I was afraid to even love again because I didn't want to give my heart to another man for him to break it like my Drew did. He stood before God and vowed to cherish and be faithful to me knowing that he didn't mean it and he abused me.

I couldn't see it then, but I see it now. Through all of this pain and everything he's put me through; God has a plan for my life. I am special. I am beautiful, even though Drew made me feel like the ugliest woman in the world. Ultimately, I've become a better person. I have my struggles, but I'm a better mother. And now, when I remarry, I will be a better wife. I can express myself in a more effective manner. And even though anger is the only emotion that was shown openly all of my life, through this experience I've learned how to love. I didn't know how to love him when I had him because it was never shown to me. I hadn't learned it. I couldn't give what I'd never had. But through this process, God started teaching me. As I learned, I began to show it to him. I took him back over 20 times and gave him all of me, even though he didn't want it. Every time I told him "Babe, I love you, come home and we can work it out, we'll get through this together," I meant it from the bottom of my heart. See, God loves us without judgment. He loved us so much that He died for us. And then He called us His "friend." He showed me that "perfect love casts out fear (1 John 4:18)," and that you can prove your love to someone by your actions and by being faithful and keeping God's commandments. I thought that it was dumb for me to stay faithful to him all of these years while he cheated on me. But God showed me that when I made a vow to my husband, I also made one to Him. And to prove my love to Him, I had to keep that vow. And I'm glad that I did. Even though I didn't want the divorce, I can walk away knowing that I honored my vows and that I did everything I could to save my marriage. I am free. And since I'm free, I'm moving on. I'm releasing this from my spirit and from my life. And I will no longer let this hurt control my life, my emotions, or my relationship with my family or my children. I had been turning down men that had a genuine interest in me and my children because in my heart I really wanted my husband, and to me, nobody compared to the "love of my life." Well, clearly that's over now. He's been in several relationships and hasn't even taken the time to heal. That makes me wonder if he ever really loved me. Even if he didn't, I loved him. But it's time for me to go on. I will not cry over him another day. And even though "you reap what you sow," I wish him happiness. I pray that grace will cover him like it's been doing for the last three years. Just know that I really loved him, I'm sorry for everything that I did, and didn't do. And I did my best.

Here is the story of the journey that I had been trapped in for several years. Travel with me as I show you what God has taken me through, and brought me out of…

Chapter 2

I Once Was Young

Growing up in a household like mine was probably one of the most challenging experiences ever. I was raised to never let anyone know if you were going through something or how your life really was. In other words, I was basically taught to put on a "front." We were very poor, but I don't think that anyone knew it. Most of my clothes were "hand me downs," or items bought from a thrift store. I can remember a time when my dress shoes were too little. And it took a while for them to be replaced. Even though the world does revolve around money, it still isn't everything. But as a child, it felt like it was. It felt like the end of the world when I wanted something and could never have what I wanted. Growing up, I vowed that if I ever had children that I would make sure to get them everything they needed, and wanted. Now that I'm an adult, I see that it's "easier said than done."

I grew up feeling like an outcast. I was the baby of the family and while I was younger, I was told that I was very spoiled, by my dad. I never knew this, but if it were true, as I got older things changed. My surroundings deemed me to feel like I was inadequate. As I began to notice my surroundings, I began to notice that there was something very different brewing inside of me. And it didn't line up with how my family members were. I used to wish that I was adopted and that one day the people that I've known as "mama" and "daddy" were not my own, but belonged to the people that were raised as my sisters and brother. I think at one point in time all children wish that they had different parents but if a child feels like this for most of his/her life, is something wrong with them? I'm not one to point the blame at anyone but I just have to say that my parents are the reason why I am the way that I am, good and most of the bad. Who told me that I was ugly? Where did my low self-esteem come from? Where did my unhappiness come from? As an adult, I have come to realize that it came from my parents. All children need their parents to tell them that they're beautiful, and that they are special, and that they can be anything that they wish they can be. Parents, if you don't validate your children, someone else will. And it will often be someone that doesn't have good intentions for them. When I was in elementary school, I was what the dumb kids called a "brainiac." I stayed on the honor roll, I won spelling bees, I was even recognized for writing a book and my family supported me. But, when I got to high school, I got a look at the real world and unfortunately, the way I was raised just wasn't it.

As a child, I'd never had a real Christmas. I didn't get to experience the joys and beauties of Christmas until I was an adult. My parents were so religious that I couldn't have a Christmas tree. Their reasoning for that was because the elders of the church felt as though when a person kneels in front of the tree to retrieve their presents, they're bowing to the tree and that you shouldn't bow to anything or anybody but God. I believe that every child wants to believe in Santa Claus. And, I believed. But for some reason, Santa never came to visit my house. I never received any of the things that I wanted for Christmas, all I got was socks, underwear and etc. I'd wanted a Christmas tree so bad and I just couldn't understand why we couldn't have it so, I went to my cousin's house one year on December 1st. She let me help her and her son put up their tree. I enjoyed it so much that it became a yearly ritual, that is, until I got older.

As previously stated, I grew up in a "super religious"

home. Because of the Pentecostal church that I grew up in, we couldn't do anything. I wore skirts every day until I was in the seventh grade. I couldn't get my ears pierced, so I did it on my own when I turned eighteen years old. I couldn't wear lip gloss. None of the women could wear make-up, young or old. We couldn't even wear toe-out or heel-out shoes. Going to the movies was strictly forbidden because we were told that there were evil spirits in the movies and that it was a bad place to go. Now that I think about it, I don't think I'd even gone bowling.

There was a shift in my childhood when my parents left the church that I was raised in and joined the church that I am a member of now. I was around the age of eleven when we joined. There were still things that we couldn't do because of religious purposes, but the rules were nothing compared to those of our former church. The church promoted a certain level of freedom to the youth that ignited an interest in all of the youth and made us want to get involved in church. We had the best youth choir in the city and it gave us an opportunity to travel every weekend to different cities and churches to sing. Because my parents were strict, there were plenty of times that I couldn't go to singing engagements. But this choir gave me something to help me stay focused on the more positive things in life. By being a part of this church and choir, I learned to become comfortable in my Christianity and to not have to feel ashamed about it because I knew that I wasn't in this alone.

Although my parents were strict, I began to blossom. I met several people and had many experiences that I wouldn't have had otherwise. I traveled to various places in the country. We met gospel celebrities and had a lot of fun. I learned a great deal of things from my friends that I probably should have learned from my family. But when you're younger, it's always easier to talk to your peers than it is to your parents. Because of the strictness of my parents, I was afraid to live and try new things in an effort to not disappoint them. After so long, this fear began to diminish. It was at the age of twelve that I had my first kiss and first boyfriend. He was a guy that went to my church. After breaking up with him, we became very good friends. I guess this was easy for us because at the age we were when we were boyfriend and girlfriend, our relationship was nothing serious. But to this day, he and I speak frequently and have remained very good friends.

Growing up, most of my friends were people that went to my church. Although I was often told that I had an "attitude," I was a good girl that loved the Lord. A disadvantage to my type of upbringing was that I was really naïve. Not being allowed to make my own mistakes and have my own experiences caused me to become curious. "Curiosity killed the cat" and spiritually, it killed me. I began to hang out with a few girls from my church. On the outside, they were good girls but on the inside? That's a different story.

I remember going to one of our youth choir's singing engagements in a different city. One of my friends drove to the engagement and instead of riding the church van back home, I rode with her. Because she and another friend of ours wanted to stop at their boyfriends' houses, we didn't get home until like 6 o'clock the next morning. My parents had been calling me all night. And I was afraid to answer the phone because I didn't want to disappoint them. Although I chose to ride with my friends, I had no control over when we left and they could care less about how many times my parents called wanting me to come home. I felt uncomfortable sitting on the couch in a stranger's living room while my friends were off in different bedrooms having sex. After that night, I vowed to never hang with them again. Needless to say, that vow didn't last long because when you've been sheltered all your life, new experiences are very appealing to the eye, and if it's something that's wrong, it's even more attractive than what's right. These girls constantly talked about sex and how good it was so quite naturally, I became curious. It really shouldn't have affected me since I'd been curious before and it never made an impact on my actions or my way of thinking. But this particular summer, my interest was piqued. It was a few days after my 19th birthday while my parents were out of town that I decided to lose my virginity. And I didn't lose it to anyone that I was currently dating. He was my ex-boyfriend. After that night, my interest dwindled because it wasn't all that it was "cracked up to be." I believed the "hype" and because of something as simple as curiosity, I lost something very dear to me that I will never be able to get back. I'd always planned to cherish it and hold on to it until marriage. Although no one forced me to do it, peer pressure pushed me over the edge. Had I held on to my purity, my life probably wouldn't be what it is today. But I know that the way my life is now was all a part of God's plan.

Because of my disappointment and my stupidity, I tried it again. Each time that I did, it was disappointing.

But like a dummy, I kept doing it. I can compare it to an addiction. You try it one time and it may not have the type of impact that you expected, so you try it again and again until you get the result that you want. Each time I came up empty, and I would go for a year or so without it and then try again to see if it would be different. Each time was pretty much the same that is, until I met Drew.

Chapter 3

A Change is Gonna Come

I can remember when I used to be happy. As a young lady, it was easy to be carefree because I had no major worries. When you're young, you don't usually listen to the things that your parents tell you. It sounds like a broken record, and sometimes you want to take that record and smash it into a wall. But, as I've grown and gotten older, I've become wiser. I was taught about God, His power and His blessings. I didn't fully understand how great He was until I had to get to know Him for myself. God will place you into a situation and allow you to get stuck so that you have no choice but to depend upon Him. He chastens them that He loves (Hebrews 12:6). And if you're disobedient, you will be punished. Everyone knows that the blessings of God are great, they are rich and favorable. But, have you ever felt like His blessings are a curse? The experience that I will discuss was simultaneously one of the best and worst experiences of my life.

I began to work at a shoe store called Layup in April of 2004. It was the beginning of summer when they were preparing for a yearly event that was known as a "tent sale." As I was ringing purchases on the register, there were tons of people in line for a chance to receive an "in-person" interview with the hopes of being hired to work in the tent. This guy approached the management table, which was located directly across from the cash registers, where I was working. He was probably the only one in line with dress clothes on, so of course he stood out amongst a bunch of people wearing jeans, t-shirts, and tennis shoes. Thank God that this was the time period when people actually walked out of the house wearing clothes rather than pajamas! While at the table, he kept eyeing me. Although he wasn't my type, he had a smile that was so bright that, to this day, I can't forget it, although I wish I could. He said "hi" to me. I spoke back and went on about my business helping customers. This guy was Drew and in the future, we had conversations about that day and he shared with me that as soon as he saw me, he knew that he'd wanted me to be his wife.

About a week later, he showed up to work. When I saw him my first thought was "I guess the dress clothes paid off." I knew up front that he was interested. But I was a little leery about talking to him. At the time, I thought that it was just because he wasn't my type. Now that I'm older, I can clearly see that wasn't it. At work, we often had group conversations and that was pretty much the only way that I would interact with him.

From afar off, he seemed to be a nice person. To me, he was a dork trying to be a thug. Which brings me to the question, why do good girls always like bad guys? It was during a group discussion at work that words were exchanged that merely piqued both of our interests and it went on like this for a little while.

One day, I was at work and it was a slow day. I just so happened to be in the manager's office looking at the work schedule. I noticed that Drew was on the schedule and that he wasn't at work. I looked up his number and called from the work phone to inform him. He stated that he didn't know that he was on the schedule and arrived about thirty minutes later. I believe that was the day that he tricked me into giving him my phone number. I don't remember what he did to get it, but it didn't hit me until after the first time he called. Drew and I hit it off really quickly. We would talk on the phone for hours. Looking back at it now, I don't remember what we were talking about because during our marriage, and even now I can't get him to have a five-minute conversation and give more than one-word responses. But, I liked him. I remember being at home one day and I was hungry. He said that he was going to bring me something to eat. I ended up changing my mind because I didn't want him to know where I lived so early in our friendship. I later found out that he had already bought my food when I'd changed my mind, and he ended up keeping the food.

It was another slow day at work and all of the employees were trying on clothes. I was trying on a pair of Apple Bottom jeans. Those jeans were expensive, but they were cute! I knew that I couldn't afford them. But, he bought them for me because he claimed that he liked the way that they looked on me. That was the first gift that Drew bought me, and we weren't even together. He was slick and I have to admit, he had game. Well, game for that day and age. Each time we talked, my heart melted. And I began to fall for him quickly.

It was a summer evening when one of our co-workers had a house party. All of the employees from Layup went to it. The only reason my parents let me go was because they knew the girl and her family from several years ago. They grew up down the street from my family before I was born. The night was wild, well for them. I just kind of sat around talking to people. But everyone else was dancing, drinking and smoking. I have to admit, I was excited when I saw him. He always knew how to dress and his cologne…well enough about that. He'd spent the entire night trying to find reasons to talk to me. Finally, he approached me to tell me that he was going to give me some money. He dug in his pocket, and at the same time he touched me. When he touched me, it felt like electricity. Or maybe it was just the few sips of whatever drink I'd sampled that night.

After the party, I'd ended up taking Drew and his best friend, Deandre, home. Man, that dude was drunk! Deandre rambled on and on during the entire ride home. Drew and I laughed at him for most of the ride, until

Deandre said "man, you should go ahead and give him a chance. Drew is a good guy and he is in LOVE with you. I'm telling you he really, really loves you." And he kept saying it over and over. I looked at Drew after what his friend had said and he looked embarrassed. After that, we rode in silence. When we got to Drew's, his first words were, "I can't believe my best friend sold me out."

"So, what he said was true?"

"Well, yes. I just didn't know how to tell you," he replied.

We sat outside talking for at least another hour. It was that night that we shared our first kiss. And the next day, I sat in church daydreaming about it.

I fell in love with him one night that we'd had a long conversation. During that conversation, he'd told me about his past and how he'd grown up. He hadn't had a mother to raise him. She was addicted to drugs.

And, she left him on his dad's doorstep in the dead of winter when he was a baby. And, he'd only had a father in his life in his early years, until he was about age 10. Then, his dad put him out and told him that he couldn't take care of him anymore because of his girlfriend and her children. After that, he'd gone to live with his grandmother and grandfather. But, eventually, they couldn't take care of him any longer either. I remember him telling me that he was homeless and slept on park benches, among other things. I won't disclose the rest of it because it's personal. Drew telling me these things inspired me to write a poem about it:

In a world stricken with grief

Pain, suffering, no sign of relief

In a time where it seems that travail will have no end

No one to call on, not even one friend

When mystery binds a broken heart

Justice sought can only be bought

When peace found turns into despair

No one to help you, no one to care

Who will cry for the child whose history taunts him daily?

Who will mend the broken heart with a healing hand before it falls apart?

Who will shed a tear when life taken for granted results in a seed being planted in toxic ground?

Health loss through stress on the chest of a man who, through experience, knows best

But, I cry…for love planted deep inside my heart and no matter how hard you try, from it I will not part

I will release a tear and drink it for water to nourish me there…where no man has ever gone before…my heart…I cry.

Shortly after I gave my heart away to Drew, my body followed. And I was all in before I'd even realized it.

Chapter 4

Uncommon Sense

Somehow Drew ended up with the lady that he calls "mama" now. She took him in and took care of him and I commend her for that. But, I have to honestly say that he probably would've turned out better if he had never met her. She never treated him like a child should be treated. And, she didn't raise him, which is something that he really needed. Because he wasn't raised right, today he is still a child, mentally. The relationship that his mother formed with him was not how it should be between a mother and a son, it was as if she was his girlfriend and is still like that today. She was controlling, and she felt like she could say who could and couldn't be in his life. She didn't like any of the women that he brought home. And, with every check that he earned, she expected to get most of it; at least that's what he told me. And, when he wasn't giving it to her, he was giving it to his siblings. And I suppose that he did give them money for all of those years, well until I came into the picture. Now, I never asked him for his money. But, he started taking his earnings and spending them on me. I received a lot of "just because" gifts. And we went on a lot of dates. As this progressed, his mother's attitude got worse and so did his siblings'. Seeing this change, I began to think that they were using him. And I told him so, this is probably another reason why his "mother" didn't like me.

I had a lot of problems with Drew. The problems that I endured started out small. When you're as naïve as I was at that age, you don't see a lot of the warning signs that are being flashed in your face. And, if you do see them, you'll often mistake their meaning for something else. Drew's true self began to come to light. But, when you're desperate to be loved, you'll sometimes settle when you know that you deserve better. At first, it was just Drew being insecure because a lot of men found me attractive. I was approached by other men quite often. Of course, he didn't like it. So, at first he would try to play if off as a joke saying things like, "Oh, I see you have a new boyfriend" or, "You have a lot of admirers." Then it changed to, "Do you know this person? Because they said they know you and they like you." Then it progressed to, "Did you know my brother before you met me? Because he said you did and that y'all slept together." Then eventually, I was outright being accused of cheating with men that I didn't even know. "So and so said that you slept with them." One thing about Drew is that he never accepts the blame for his mistakes so everything that happened was not his fault but is someone else's. He came to me one day and told me

"My family said that you're talking to this guy. And he drives a gray car, an old-school model. He works at this place and he looks like this."

I didn't know anyone that fit that description so I told him "no."

He said "Are you sure? Because that's what they told me."

"No, I don't know anyone like that."

So, a day went by. And he brought it up again. "My family said that they saw you with him yesterday. And, someone I know heard you talking about it at the salon."

Well, I had already told him that I didn't know the guy and all of this was indeed a lie because I never went to the salon to get my hair done. I did it myself. So even though I knew he was lying, I felt like I was being set up.

Then he says, "They left his phone number on my dresser and told me to call him and talk to him. So, I did.

I asked him if he knew you. And he said "yes." I asked him to describe you and he did. He told me exactly what you look like, what kind of car you drive, and where you work. And, my family said that you're lying about knowing him so they are going to set you up because you're going out with him this weekend."

I said, "Ok, this should be interesting because I really don't know this guy." So, the next night came and I asked him, "What happened to me going out with this guy?"

He said "They said that they were going to set you up but they changed their minds and didn't do it."

"Who is this "family" that you're talking about?"

"My mom and Lula; who my friends and I often referred to as Dogface." Dogface, which I later found out, is Drew's ex-girlfriend.

The funny thing about the situation is that I spent all of my free time with Drew. When I wasn't at work or church, then wherever I was, he was there also. And, no wonder this situation didn't make any sense because his mom and ex-girlfriend had been trying to break us up since we'd been together. These two people had been a problem in our relationship since the VERY beginning. Drew and I had talked as friends before we'd gotten together so I'd seen this girl around before. She'd always pick him up from work whether he wanted her to or not. One night, she pulled up to pick him up from work. I'd worked an earlier shift this day, so my co-workers told me what had happened. He saw her but went to get in the car with someone else. When he did that, she made a scene, yelling out his name, and acting crazy. I asked him who she was and he told me that she was just a friend. So, I left it at that.

About a month later, I went with Drew to his family's house on Christmas. His family was there and they were acting really nice. Later, she showed up with his sister. His sister was acting "funny" and Dogface was too. I'm thinking "Ok, she's weird." His mom introduced us "Um, this is Drew's friend Cassandra." And Dogface said, "I know her. Yup, I know her, while nodding her head." I looked at her like she was crazy because just because you've seen me around doesn't mean that you know me. Shortly after, they started passing out gifts. And his family made a BIG deal about him giving me my gift. Two of his cousins went into the room giggling and making a scene, and came back out with a bag from Kay Jewelers. He grabbed the bag and handed it to me. Then he gave his mom her gift. So, we opened them. Well, my gift was a diamond tennis bracelet. And before I could react to it, Dogface got up and stormed out of the room with an "attitude" and his mom followed her and they started yelling and arguing. And, of course, I wasn't supposed to hear it but they were loud enough. After he opened his gift from me, which was a really expensive outfit, he asked if we could leave because there was too much drama. After we had left, I asked him "What was wrong with your mom?"

He said, "Oh, she was mad because she thought your gift was more expensive than hers."

I said, I asked him "Why would she think something like that?" "And what was wrong with your friend?" After all, his mom's gift was nice, and I'd helped him pick it out the night before. And, her gift was NOT cheap.

He said, "I don't know."

And he wasn't being honest with me. Later I found out that he was right about his mom. But, that was also when I found out that Dogface wasn't just a friend, but was his ex-girlfriend. I asked him why he wasn't honest with me about it. His reason was because it had only lasted for not even a month and didn't mean anything. I didn't press the issue but very soon after that I found out that although the relationship wasn't long, she still had feelings for him and those feelings soon turned into obsession. This girl would NOT go away. She practically lived in his house. Drew was using her for her car. And, she was stupid enough to let him. He would take her car to meet me places and to bring me anything that I asked for, which at the time I didn't know. But, she was also taking him places that he wanted to go. Well, as his girlfriend, I felt like this was disrespectful so I asked him not to do it anymore and to leave her alone altogether. It took him a minute to stop but eventually, he did, or at least he "said" he did. By then I had already fallen in love with him and still didn't know that he was a habitual liar.

I tried my best to show him how doing these things was disrespectful but he just didn't see it. I knew then that he didn't understand because he never really had anyone to teach him this. So, things that were just common sense to me didn't always make sense to him. I knew that his hanging out with his ex-girlfriend was disrespectful. But I, like most women, felt like I could change him. And when I look back on it now, staying with him was the biggest mistake of my life. Although

I was very mature for my age, I decided to act dumb and play these games with him. I just wanted to show him how it felt. So, I called my ex-boyfriend, Jamal. I had Jamal pick me up for work and take me home, even though I had a car. Drew found out about it and he got upset. I asked him how he felt about it. He said that he didn't like it. But, did he stop riding around with his ex-girlfriend? No.

It was a Sunday night. I was at home, talking to Drew on the phone. He told me that he was getting ready to go to the store. He didn't have a car so I asked him how he was getting there. He told me that he was driving his neighbor's car (he said that she was like his sister). I asked him what color the car was, I don't know why but I guess I was just curious. He told me that it was white. When I got off of the phone with him, I received a call from one of my friends asking me if Drew has a sister with a car. I said yeah, why?

"Because, I just saw him driving a burgundy car

with a fat girl with nappy hair in the passenger seat."

"Really?"

"Yeah. They were driving down Martin Luther King Street."

"Oh, that wasn't his sister but thanks for calling."

"Uh oh. Did I just open up a can of worms?"

"Yes you did. But I am so thankful for it."

What that friend had just told me, without knowing, was that he was driving his ex-girlfriend's car and that she was with him. I got off of the phone with that friend and called Drew. He didn't answer. He never ignored my calls so I called him back. I called at least three times before he picked up."

"Hello?"

"Where are you?"

"I'm on my way to the store. I just told you that."

"Who are you with?"

"Nobody, I'm by myself."

"You just gone lie to me like that?"

"I'm not lying."

"Whose car are you in?"

"I'm in my sister's car."

"Would that sister be Dogface?"

"What? What are you talking about?"

"Somebody just called me and told me that they saw you driving her car and that she's with you. So why are you lying? And why are you in her car?"

"Because I didn't have no other way to the store."

"Well then you should've walked."

"Man, whatever. I'll call you back."

I am very ashamed to say it, but it didn't stop there. Although it didn't seem like it, we did spend time apart.

He spent a lot of time doing dumb things and I spent a lot of time either seeking revenge or trying to get him to see the error in his ways. We were definitely unequally yoked. But it was one particular evening after I'd left my ex-boyfriend's house, when I truly realized that although Drew wasn't perfect, he was still the man that I wanted to be with. I got very close to cheating on Drew that night. But before it went too far, I left and went home.

Shortly after, we were engaged to be married. I remember Drew asking my parents for my hand in marriage, but I honestly don't remember the proposal. I do know that we hadn't been able to afford an engagement ring, so he gave me a promise ring. My family was so excited about the engagement. My mom actually went around introducing him as her "son-in-law." It was hilarious to me because we weren't even married yet! She has never really liked anyone that I brought home. So it was weird to me.

The engagement was supposed to be a time of bliss. But, for me it was similar to what we call "hell." I absolutely hated his family. They weren't his blood relatives and I was glad about it because they were the messiest people that I had ever met in my entire life. But, he wanted them involved in our wedding. We couldn't get them to show up to their fittings for the wedding attire. They would sit right there underneath his mother listening to her foolishness and creating drama. When I say they created drama, I mean his ex-girlfriend too. But, outside of family drama, during the engagement, he'd gotten his act together. Well, for a short time.

Chapter 5

My Life Shattered

Getting involved with Drew had already drastically changed my life. Was it really that drastic, you might ask? Yes, because I had been sheltered all of my life. And being as naïve as I was, I'd never experienced half of the things that I'd experienced since I'd been with him. I spent a lot of time trying to understand why people do the things that they do. Even now, sometimes I find myself trying to find an answer to this question. But the reality is the answer to this question we may never know.

It was during the engagement that I ended up pregnant. Naturally, becoming a mother is a joyous experience. But, this experience was designed for women that are married. This information was drilled into my head daily. So of course, after growing up in church, it's not something that can easily be let go. Although I was engaged to be married, there is no justification for having premarital sex and definitely no justification for having children out of wedlock. Imagine the humiliation and receiving thrown accusations of being an embarrassment. An embarrassment to whom, you might ask? I was an embarrassment to my family, not only natural but spiritual. My family means a lot to me and I never meant to disappoint anyone. It happens sometimes because we're human. There is no one that is perfect but God. And the bible says "he who is without sin, let him cast the first stone (John 8:7)." Although the word said it, not many people follow it.

Before I'd told anyone that I was pregnant, I wanted

an abortion. I contemplated on this day and night. Eventually, I'd made up in my mind that that was what I was going to do. I had so much to lose. I was still in school. Yes, it was a University but everyone knows that college students are usually broke. I had a job, but it was measly with low pay and no benefits. This was not a condition that children were welcome in. Although I was engaged to be married, that didn't bring much hope because my fiancé had a measly job also. But the difference was, he was terrible at managing money, and to this day, he still is. Since he was partly responsible for my being impregnated, I had a talk with him to tell him my decision. It didn't go so well.

I remember going up to our job while he was at work with the pregnancy test in tow. I proceeded to tell him that I wanted an abortion and why. That was probably the worse thing that I could have said to him because of his childhood. Well, at least he'd made it seem that way. By the end of the conversation, I'd actually let him talk me into maintaining the pregnancy. And, I believed him when he said that he'd be a father to his children because he didn't want his child to be raised like he was. Why did I let him talk me out of it?

Shortly after I found out that I was pregnant, I entered the hospital threatening a miscarriage. The process of stopping the symptoms is not only long, but tedious. I can still remember lying on the ultrasound table when the nurse announced, "You're having twins." When the shock hit me, it was like someone had smashed a brick into my face. Soon after, the shock was replaced with anger. I didn't plan to get pregnant. I honestly believe that no one, in their right mind, actually plans it, with the exception of married couples. Plus, I was on the birth control shot! There were so many emotions that should have been running through my head but anger was most prevalent. And, it prevailed throughout the entire pregnancy. It was hard enough to tell my family that I was pregnant, but to tell them that I was pregnant with twins was extremely difficult. The first person that I called was my mom and like me, she was very upset. She didn't have much to say but no one likes to be kicked when they're down so, her reaction was not needed. Unlike everyone else, the father of my children was ecstatic. For what, I don't know. And that is a question that has still gone unanswered. Yes, children are a blessing but they're not meant to be had outside of a marital covenant for a reason. My life has proven that. The pregnancy itself was a blow to me but this twin thing was a sucker punch. After leaving the hospital, life continued, not as I knew it but as it was going to be. At the time, I became content. After all that's what the apostle Paul says, right? That didn't take long to change.

> "Not that I speak in respect of want: for I have learned, in whatsoever state I am, therewith to be content."
>
> Philippians 4:1 KJV

Ever since I was I child, I knew that I didn't want any children. At least not outside of marriage, and my wanting an abortion was probably the best thing that I could've done in my life. By the time I was six weeks pregnant, I knew that I was in this alone. But, since we were engaged to be married, I couldn't help but to be hopeful. When you're marrying someone, you begin to have high expectations of them, whether you've accepted their flaws or not. And by the time I was six weeks pregnant, I'd already told people that I was expecting so I couldn't get an abortion, although the thought still crossed my mind everyday. So, I began to think of ways that I could pull it off. Um, let's see, I can get an abortion and pretend that I had a miscarriage. At the time, I didn't think that I could pull it off but now that I look at it, it could have worked…and worked well. And, I hate to say it, but I should've done it. You will soon find out why.

As my pregnancy progressed, so did my feelings,

temper, and everything else. Even though I very much took part in creating the babies, I was very upset when I found out that I was pregnant. For one, I was on the birth control shot. So you mean to tell me that not only did I get pregnant, I was pregnant with twins? The pregnancy changed life as I knew it. It caused a lot of my relationships to fail, those that he hadn't already destroyed. While I was three months pregnant, I moved out of my mother's house because at the time there were at least 9 people living in my house. It was my father, mother, sister, brother, sister-in-law, three of her children and her grandson. And, since I was pregnant with twins, I experienced double of everything; double the morning sickness, pain, depression, emotional breakdowns, and attitude. Whatever notions you have about pregnancy, throw it in there because I was experiencing it. I hated living in a house with so many people. Everything I ate came right back up. It had gotten to the point where I had to take a Benadryl at least twice a day just to be able to hold my food down. And, with there being a lot of people in the house, that made it so that every time I needed to go to the restroom, someone was in there. I couldn't deal with it anymore so I moved out. Although it made life harder, it was one of the best things that I could've done in my life and I never plan on moving back into my parent's house.

Now, I've been poor all of my life and no, I'm not bragging on it because it's something that I'm not proud of, and it seems as though I've had no control over it. But, ever since I'd gotten pregnant, I'd been even poorer than before. I honestly didn't think that it could get any worse, but unfortunately, it did. I got put on bed rest early in the pregnancy because I was threatening a miscarriage and, even though I didn't want to, I followed the doctor's orders. I left my job and ended up on state aide. I received $305 a month in cash and $400 in food stamps. I don't know anyone that can survive off of that amount of money a month but I didn't have a choice. My car note was $200 a month. And, because

My Life Shattered

I wasn't making anything, I didn't have rent; I lived in income-based apartments. My phone bill was $55 a month and I was nowhere near prepared for the babies, they didn't have anything. The only way that I was able to get my babies a crib and a dresser for their room was because although the doctor said that I couldn't work, he allowed me to go to school. I used the money that I got from school to buy those things, and that was all that I could do.

When we'd first moved into the apartment, I was 3 months pregnant. My fiancé's name was on the lease and at the time, he wasn't employed so the rent stayed the same. The next month, he got a job in the mall. Because his name was on the lease, we had to report the change in income and they raised my rent to $56.

He was the reason that we had rent in the first place, so he agreed to pay it. Sad to say, he never did, NOT ONCE! I paid rent for about 2-3 months, and was living off of nothing. I got fed up because I really couldn't afford it so I made him sign a paper saying that he'd moved out, I got it notarized and took his name off of the lease and told them that he'd moved out because I couldn't keep paying it. The truth is, technically, he was still supposed to be living with me. But he really wasn't. For whatever reason, he'd decided to go back home to his mom's. Well, at least that's where he said that he was. I didn't realize it at the time, but this was going to become a pattern.

It didn't take long for the pregnancy to progress to the high-risk category. I spent a lot of time in the hospital threatening miscarriages. I ended up having to drop out of school. It got to the point where the doctor said "if there's a piece of paper on the floor, don't bend over and pick it up. Leave it there, or you'll go into labor." This was a problem for me because my fiancé was a slob. He was still in and out of the house, when he came, it looked like a hurricane hit the place. I was so depressed, and so embarrassed. One particular time when I was approximately seven months pregnant, my mom and sister came over and he had clothes all over the living room. I still remember the look on my sister's face when she had to move a pile of stuff just to sit on the sofa. I apologized for the mess and explained the situation. Her reaction was, "So, HE did all of this? I know you've never lived like this." He'd leave dirty dishes lying around. And, I remember having to create a path just to get across the floor. So when the doctor told me not to bend over a pick up a piece of paper, I remember saying "but you don't understand. He has left my house in shambles." I argued with him for like five minutes. Needless to say, he was right. But being forced to helplessly live like that is the reason why I am such a "neat-freak today." My family calls me "anal retentive," but having to suffer like that definitely did some damage to me mentally.

The further along in the pregnancy I got, the worse it got. I'd be in the hospital for sometimes two weeks at a time. During these times, Drew was really supportive. He'd spend day and night with me. Then, he would have those spurts where he'd want to run off again. It kind of reminded me of a drug addict. I remember a time that I hadn't seen him for a while. I don't know how I ended up talking to his friend that had kind of hooked us up. But, whenever I needed to reach him, the guy would call "Dogface." Well, why would he need to call her? Wasn't he staying at his mom's? There would be times when he would call me in the middle of the night freaking out and wanting me to come get him. I'd get my pregnant butt up, out of the bed and drive all the way across town to get him. One night while I was on my way to get him, a cop car almost ran into me. So naturally, I hit my brakes. This cop actually had the nerve to pull me over after almost smashing into me talking about I was speeding. I said, "No, I wasn't speeding. I hit my brakes because you almost hit me." After I said that, he decided to let me go. I'm sure it was because I was right, or maybe just because he realized that I was pregnant.

Near the end of the pregnancy, I would be at the doctor's office four days a week. I'd have an ultrasound every week. Then there was the stress test. Sometimes, I'd just have to sit for an hour everyday for the nurses to monitor the babies' heartbeats. This was during one of those times where he hadn't been around. He had started this job working weird hours, supposedly. And he was very secretive about it. He'd told me the name of the company, and luckily a phone number. I didn't know what department he worked in, what he did; I knew practically nothing. One day, before I went to the hospital for another test, I called the number that he gave me and somehow ended up speaking to his supervisor. I told her that I was Drew's fiancée and that I was pretty far along in the pregnancy. I told her that I'd been having complications and wondered if it would be okay for me to call him if there were an emergency. Surprisingly, she was really nice and supportive. She told me her name and gave me the direct extension to reach her. Shortly after the conversation, I went to have my test done. During the test, they couldn't find the second baby's heartbeat. I'd gone to the doctor the day before and he'd told me to tell the technician to notify him as soon as I got there and to tell him everything that's happening with the babies. As soon as he picked up the phone he said, "It's the twins, isn't it?" After the technician got off the phone, she said to me "You're about to have an emergency c-section." They escorted me to a room to get me ready. On my way to the room, I called my family and they came immediately. As soon as I got to the room, I picked up the phone and called Drew's supervisor. As soon as she realized that it was me, she said "it's time already? Ok, I'll go get him." She put me on hold and went to get Drew. When he got on the phone, I told him what was about to happen. He said, "Ok, I'll get there as soon as I can." It turns out that he'd called around and didn't have a ride. My mom didn't want to leave the hospital to get him because she was going to go into surgery with me and didn't want to miss it. He missed the birth of our babies. I was a little disappointed. But after I got out of surgery, he was at the hospital. His uncle had brought him. He got to see the babies before I did and he was so excited. The second baby got sent to the Neonatal Intensive Care Unit (NICU) immediately because he had trouble breathing. I didn't get a chance to see him until the next day. The first baby, they brought to see me for about three minutes and because he was having trouble breathing too, they took him to NICU too. I was so devastated that I couldn't stop crying. But, Drew was there being supportive, which was a good thing because I didn't feel so alone.

When I took the babies home, I went to my mom's so that I could have some help. Drew claimed that he was working and wasn't around much. When he did come, I was so tired and in pain that my parents let him stay the night on the couch in the den. I took the babies in there with him to let them wake him up all night with their crying. Coping was hard. Because of my incision, when the babies cried it took me like five minutes to get up because of the pain. It was nice to have him there to help.

After a while, I got tired of being away from home. And, I missed my fiancé. We took the babies home, and for a few weeks things were ok. But, like my life, that quickly changed.

Chapter 6

Shambles...

Everything seemed to be going okay until one day I came home and saw some of Drew's things gone and that he had left his key on the table. Naturally, I became curious as to what was going on. We hadn't had a fight so I had no clue what was happening. I called him. I asked him why did he leave his key and take his belongings. He replied, "I didn't think that you would want me there anymore." When I inquired further, he said that he had something to tell me and that he would talk to me soon.

I went about my business bathing my babies and getting them ready for bed. I was already uneasy. But things got worse when I received a phone call from his mother.

"Have you talked to my son?"

"Um, for a minute. Why?"

"So, he didn't tell you?"

"Tell me what?"

"Dogface is pregnant. That big whore is pregnant."

"What?" And instantly, I started crying. In seconds, my world was shattered and my life began to flash before my eyes.

"Yes, she's pregnant. And you better not cry over him. He's scum and he's not worth it."

"Why would you tell me this?" I asked.

"I told him that if he didn't tell you then I would." Then she started running off at the mouth.

"I have to go," I replied. And I hung up on her. I stood in the bathroom for an amount of time that I'm unsure of. My sadness instantly turned to anger. My thoughts began to change, I have two children that I don't want and this bastard has the nerve to cheat on me and get that whore pregnant? This nigga ruined my life! A few minutes later, he came knocking on the apartment door. When he saw my face, "Mom told you?" were his first words. I don't remember anything other than him on his knees begging me not to leave him. I was so hurt that I couldn't even think straight. I remember calling my mom to ask her to keep the babies because I couldn't deal with them at the moment. She came over for like 30 minutes, but wouldn't take them. I was upset, alone and couldn't do a thing about it. This was one of the worst experiences in my life. I wished that I could go back in time and change everything I'd done to get myself into this predicament.

Over time, my anger progressed. I began to plot and scheme on things that I could do to get rid of this girl. In the midst of my plotting, Drew's mom thought that it would be best to move him out of town so that he could get a fresh start and prepare for me and the babies to move with him. She helped him move to Kentucky. Even though I still loved him, I was pissed off. And I wanted revenge. So, I decided to "hook up" with someone else. Now let me give you a disclaimer. "Two wrongs do not make a right." It's not even in my nature to lie and cheat, but anger will have you do some stupid things. After I slept with someone else, I called him and told him. Yes, he was angry but I see now that it hurt me more than it hurt him, and it also hurt the other person that I included.

Because I was still hurting, I kept planning. On the night that I was going to follow through with my plan, I received a telephone call saying that Dogface was admitted into the hospital and that the baby was born early. When her baby died, I remember being on the telephone with my best friend and her telling me, "See, God said He doesn't need you to seek revenge. Vengeance is His, and He has it all in His hands. He took care of this situation without you." I hate to admit, I was happy when her baby died. Ever since the day that I found out that she was pregnant, she became a huge problem. She would call my house all hours of the day and night. She would pop up at my house unannounced trying to start drama. She had people calling my house for her. It was bad enough that she knowingly screwed my fiancé, but to harass me? This girl had a serious problem. And Drew had the nerve to be afraid of her, even though he'd slept with her. I remember one time while I was at work. He was home alone with the babies. She showed up unannounced knocking on the door, yelling and trying to start some mess. He called his mom and brother saying, "She's here acting crazy and I don't know what to do." He was afraid to open the door. Needless to say, it didn't end there. But after the loss of her baby, she stayed away from me.

Even though Drew & I were living in sin, that was still my fiancé and I hate liars and cheaters. It was unfair that he ruined my life, and I felt like he had to give to me and our children what was due to us, him. He would constantly lead me on. I remember a number of times when he'd tell me that he was on the bus on his way home and for me to come get him from the bus station. After my second time going to get him and he wasn't there, I stopped going.

Eventually, we started to grow apart. He kept lying and cheating so I ended the relationship. Eventually, I started dating other people and didn't have time to talk to him, or entertain his foolishness. It was in a few short months that I rekindled a relationship with an old friend that I'd dated previously. I was so happy. And Drew hated it. He would come to Michigan without announcing it. He would be outside of my apartment telling me what cars were parked where and etc. I remember him telling me that he was in town and that he needed a ride. Of course I didn't believe him, because he'd said that before. I remember coming home one day to find him sitting on my porch. So, I left him with the babies so that I could go to work. I continued to see the guy that I was seeing.

Eventually, Drew ended up moving back to Michigan. I was over him so I didn't want to be bothered. He claimed that he didn't have anywhere to stay so I let him stay in the guest room, not in my bedroom with me. He would keep me up all night with his phone ringing, drama and etc. I remember one day at six o'clock in the morning, I heard something that sounded like a wounded dog howling. It startled me out of my sleep. I got up to see what it was, and he was laying in the middle of the kitchen floor, on the telephone, crying, and saying, "She don't love me no more. She won't take me back." When he realized that I was in the room, he crawled over to me and grabbed my legs crying, "Please take me back. I'm so sorry I hurt you." Well, I was sleepy and I didn't want him to wake the babies so I replied, "Can you keep it down? I don't want you to wake the babies." I turned and walked away and went back to bed. As I ascended the stairs, he started howling again. Now that I look back at it, it was really pitiful. I felt that he was sorry, but I didn't trust him. So, I dealt with him with a "long handled spoon."

Despite anything that I did, he wouldn't leave my house. He stayed there for a year. Eventually, I moved to a different apartment complex. He helped me move, and never left there either. Over the course of two years, he became a better person, or so I thought. Even though we weren't together, he kept a job, he paid bills, helped keep the house clean, helped with the children, even made an attempt at cooking every now and then. We were happy. We rarely had any arguments. I guess it was because we weren't together, even though everyone thought that we were. Truthfully, I just loved sleeping with him. We both got what we wanted (sex) without being fully committed. We were content…and in sin. Well, I was content but he wasn't. He begged me to take him back and to marry him for an entire two years. If I'd had any sense, I wouldn't have done it at all. Neither he nor I were ready for marriage, but it happened so fast.

Chapter 7

Engaged Again?

I knew all along that this was the person that I wanted to spend the rest of my life with, or at least I thought I knew. But, I wasn't ready to be married and neither was he. If I could do things differently, I would have waited to get married. But, we can't change our past, only our future. We had decided to get married before this time. The previous wedding was postponed because I ended up pregnant.

When we decided to get married a second time, he had been begging me to marry him for two years. And had it not been for me thinking about my children and their future, I would have made him beg me a lot more.

It had been Drew's lifelong dream to go to the Air Force. When he finally decided that he wanted to go, we met with a few recruiters and they had all said the same thing. If he goes to the Air Force and leaves you with children these young, he won't be able to get in without being married to you. While we were in the recruiter's office, he took preliminary tests and physicals, and he passed them. The recruiter also scheduled him for the ASVAB test and a physical while we were at his office. We then proceeded to discuss marriage. The Air Force recruiter enforced a time frame that we had to follow in order for him to get everything completed in time for his departure. Drew kept telling me how badly that he wanted to go. We were in constant contact with the recruiter and Drew couldn't wait to get started either. All in all, I felt like I was forced into marriage. Within a week, we had a scheduled date for Drew to leave. We started marriage counseling immediately, set a date, and planned a wedding within two months.

I had already had my wedding dress from the first time we'd planned to get married. We'd also previously picked out a wedding cake so all we had to do in that area was call the cake lady and pay a deposit. In a matter of two months, I had gotten fitted for my dress to get it altered. I got the bridesmaids in to get sized for their dresses. We chose colors, got the rings, secured a photographer, hired a decorator for the church sanctuary, bought decorations to decorate the reception hall, bought flowers and had the bouquets made, got a band & etc.

We had a counseling session once a week, with the exception of the last week. While in marriage counseling, the pastor sat with us and discussed scriptures and God's design for marriage. During each session, he stressed the importance of fidelity in marriage. The pastor, Pastor Austin, gave each of us a bible to follow along. He went over many scriptures. But the ones that he stressed were as follows:

> "Ye have heard that it was said by them of old time, Thou shalt not commit adultery: But I say unto you, That whosoever looketh on a woman to lust after her hath committed adultery with her already in his heart."
>
> Matthew 5:27-28

> "It has been said, Whosoever shall put away his wife, let him give her a writing of divorcement: But I say unto you, That whosoever shall put away his wife, saving for the cause of fornication, causeth her to commit adultery: and whosoever shall marry her that is divorced committeth adultery."
>
> Matthew 5:31-32 KJV

> "And Jesus answered and said unto them, For the hardness of your heart he wrote you this precept. But from the beginning of the creation God made them male and female. For this cause shall a man leave his father and mother, and cleave to his wife; And they twain

shall be one flesh: so then they are
no more twain, but one flesh. What
therefore God hath joined together, let
not man put asunder."

Mark 10:2-9 KJV

"And unto the married I command, yet
not I, but the Lord, Let not the wife
depart from her husband: But and if she
depart, let her remain unmarried, or be
reconciled to her husband: and let not
the husband put away his wife."

1 Corinthians 7:10-11 KJV

Pastor Austin discussed all of the scriptures with us in detail. He had read the entire 7th chapter of 1st Corinthians, but added emphasis on verses 10-11. He explained to us that when you get married, you don't just leave your father and mother, you leave your sister, brother, aunts, uncles, friends, ex-boyfriends/ex-girlfriends and etc. He stressed that marriage is sacred. It is a covenant and that it is not meant to be taken lightly. He asked if we understood the things we'd discussed and allowed us to ask questions if we needed clarification. Each session was pretty much the same.

I had prayed and asked God whether or not I should marry Drew. I wasn't clear on the answer that I was receiving from God. I'm sure that it was partly because I was conflicted. I wanted my children to have both of their parents in the home and for us to do that without living in sin. And I wanted to do things right. Even though I'd been praying, I wasn't sure if I should marry him. So I called Pastor Austin and told him what I was feeling. I explained to him that I was unsure and asked him whether or not he saw any reason why I shouldn't marry him. I asked him to pray with me about it and if he saw any reason why I shouldn't marry him, to tell me and I wouldn't do it. He agreed to pray with me on this.

While still in prayer, we continued our counseling sessions and finalizing the wedding plans. One day, Drew and I were out running errands. Drew was driving. While he was driving, I received a call from

Pastor Austin. I answered the telephone. After saying our greetings he said, "I was just calling to see if you're doing ok."

"Yes, I'm doing ok," I replied.

"He hasn't told you, has he?"

"Told me what?"

"I'll tell you what. Call me after you talk to him."

I got off of the telephone and asked Drew what he was talking about. I remember that we were leaving Corunna Road where it turns into Court Street. He pulled over into the gas station so that we could talk.

"What is it that you have to tell me?" I asked Drew.

"Well, I made a mistake. I slept with Dogface."

"You did what?!" I yelled.

"Well, I didn't actually sleep with her. I started and I felt guilty so I stopped and left."

"Why would you do something like this?"

"I promise it was a mistake but it will never happen again." And he went on and on about how sorry he was.

At this point, I was done talking. I definitely didn't have anything else to say so I shut all the way down. We sat there in silence for at least thirty minutes. I felt like an idiot. I had just spent almost $3,000 total on this wedding, which is all of the money that I had and couldn't get any of it back. I was pissed off. Finally, Drew decides to start driving again, heading home. While we were riding, I picked up the telephone and called Pastor Austin back.

"So he told you?"

"Yes, he did."

"Do you know what you're going to do?"

"I have no idea what I'm going to do."

"Yeah, this really stinks."

"I'm going to think about it, but can we still have the

counseling session so that we can discuss it?"

"Sure, we can."

Then we got off of the telephone. I'm telling you, this really ruined everything. Putting things into perspective now, this was my answer from God. God was telling me not to marry him. But of course we all have a tendency to be hard-headed. I was thinking about all of the money that I'd spent that was non-refundable. All of the girls had bought their dresses. I felt guilty because that would have been a waste of people's hard-earned money. He'd even spent over $2,000 on my ring. Truthfully, we had to downsize my ring because we needed the money to pay for other things for the wedding and so that we could at least go out of town for our "honeymoon." But why did I feel guilty? I'm not the one that cheated. I had so many thoughts running through my head. So, instead of listening to the voice of God, I was calculating loss not once considering that marrying him might create another loss in the future.

When we went to our counseling session that week, there was definitely tension in the air. In the session, Pastor Austin asked me again what I wanted to do. I told him that I was conflicted. I don't think I gave him my reasoning in detail. But, I remember sitting in the chair envisioning everything that I would lose if I walked away from the wedding. I didn't want to face the humiliation. Not to mention, the fact that he wouldn't be able to go to the Air Force and if he couldn't do that, what about my children's future? How would we be able to guarantee a good life for our children? I was envisioning these things while the pastor was talking to Drew, so clearly I wasn't paying attention to anything that was being said. But I will say that I believe at this point, both the pastor and I were sick of this crap because we'd been there before. So the pastor reiterated everything that we'd gone over in the previous sessions. He repeated all of the scriptures on adultery. He again stressed the importance of being faithful to your spouse in marriage. By the end of the session, both Drew and I decided to go on with the wedding and the pastor agreed to perform the ceremony.

Let me just say this and hear me well. When God gives you an out, take it! Everything that He does, He does it for a reason. When He closes a door, don't question Him. Perhaps it means that He has something better for you. This was my chance to walk away from bondage and because of my stupidity and disobedience, I've had to suffer the consequences.

Chapter 8

Wedding Bells

Time flew by after that very tense counseling session. Now, it was the day before the wedding. My wedding planner and I had spent most of the day at the church decorating the fellowship hall. We had to make sure that the decorators got in to decorate the sanctuary and that they were doing it the way that I requested. In the midst of the chaos, I had forgotten to eat. Even though we were super busy, we stuck together and saw it through until the end.

During the wedding rehearsal, the wedding coordinator spoke with everyone to give them a rundown of how things were going to flow. Everyone got into their places. Everyone was kind of joking around so when it was time for us to practice our vows, Pastor Austin made Drew vow "to be faithful" like 5 times. Everyone thought that the pastor was joking but in reality, he wasn't.

The day of the wedding started out serene. I woke up alone. Drew stayed the night with his uncle and the boys had stayed with him. I went about my business getting my hair done and making a few last minute runs. While at the salon, one of my friends called to check on me. The only time I'd talked to Drew was to see how he and the boys were doing.

I arrived at the church before any of the wedding party, with the exception of the wedding coordinator. I sat in the room alone and nervous while she handled last minute things. In a matter of minutes, serenity turned into chaos. All of the girls were getting dressed, doing makeup, taking pictures & etc. While the men that were in the wedding were just relaxing. During the preparation, I kept a smile on my face while on the inside, I was terrified.

Finally, it was time to start the wedding. The music began to play. All of the girls left me in the room alone to get in their places. His mom came into the room to talk to me. While she was talking to me, I burst out in tears. I don't think she had a clue why I was crying. I decided to put tissue in the front of my dress in case I had another crying spell. I got it together and she left to go to her seat. While I was alone in the room, I remember standing next to the door looking out of the window feeling as though I was making a mistake. I was terrified and I wanted to run. I had doubts. I loved Drew, but could I really spend the rest of my life with him knowing the things he'd done to me in the past? A lot of thoughts flooded my mind. Before I could do anything, it was time for me to walk down the aisle.

It was the wedding coordinator's idea to have everyone stay seated while I walked down the aisle so that everyone could see me better. The idea was different, but it made me more nervous. I was shaking the entire way down the aisle. All eyes were on me and I wanted to cry again. When I saw Drew, he had the brightest smile on his face. He seemed really happy. It only eased my fears a little bit though. While the soloist was singing, I took a look around. I noticed people in his family, who he wanted there and I didn't. They were gossiping, whispering and texting. Later I found out that they were texting Dogface and rubbing the wedding in her face, like messy people do. I shed tears as we recited our vows. As I released the tears, the nervousness began to leave.

Finally, we were pronounced husband and wife. As we walked down the aisle, I started to feel better. While taking our wedding pictures, I remember standing next to Drew thinking, "Finally, we get to spend our lives together and I don't have to share him with any other women." Naturally, that's how it's supposed to be. Was I asking for too much?

The rest of the night flew by. And we were exhausted. His "godparents" had missed the wedding and they wanted Drew and I to come by. We stopped over there before we went home. I met the rest of the family. They were all very nice and supportive. After leaving there, we went home to change clothes. His mother, sister, and god sister followed us home. When we got there, he had forgotten to carry me over the threshold and they made us go outside and do it over. It was hilarious. The soloist at the wedding had blessed us with a hotel room for us to stay in the night of our wedding. So, we got our bags and left the house to head to the hotel. We were really excited.

We spent the night in the hotel. The next morning, we got up and ate breakfast together. We had a lot of laughs.

After breakfast, we ran one last errand to make sure that the car was safe to drive on the expressway and headed to Ohio for a few days for our honeymoon. Neither of us could believe that we were married. It was exciting and surreal at the same time. On our honeymoon, we had fun. We got plenty of rest. And we enjoyed each other's company. Before long, it was time to go home and get back to real life. It didn't take long for reality to hit.

Chapter 9

Marital Fits…Oops Bliss

The first two months of marriage were blissful. We'd been living together for so long so that was the same. The only thing that we really had to adjust to was realizing that we were no longer living in sin, as we'd done for so long.

Two months into our marriage, Drew started cheating again. I started to hate him and seriously regretted marrying him. I'd had no proof in hand, but I was sure that he was cheating. His mother had bought him a cell phone so that we could stay in touch with each other. She and my family were very supportive of our marriage. When he first got the cell phone, we would plug both of our cell phones in on the night stand to charge and leave them there overnight. After a while, Drew would start spending nights away from home claiming that he was at his god brother's house. When I would ask him why he didn't come home, he would reply that he didn't know. Drew would take his cell phone and charge it downstairs in the living room so that I couldn't look at it…not that I would have. But a person's actions can raise suspicions. So I was definitely suspicious. Two months into our marriage, we were back in marriage counseling. Even though I'd talked to people about how unhappy I was, no one knew why because I never said it. I oftentimes rationalized rather than giving people an open reason because being married to an adulterer was humiliating. So, the pastor was the only person I had talked to about my suspicions.

Looking back, one of the biggest mistakes that

Drew and I both made was involving other people in our marriage. We often sought advice from the wrong people. One particular person that I had talked to planted the seed of divorce into my head. Now, this person has never been married, doesn't have any children and couldn't even relate to any of the things that I was going through so they were definitely the wrong person to talk to. Drew began talking to people that he shouldn't have been talking to either. A different person told him to leave me after he went to them complaining about never being able to spend money on himself because I wanted to use it towards bills, not only that but we had two children that needed to be taken care of. Who takes on a family but doesn't want to take care of them? This person that he talked to had never been married either. And none of these people that we were talking to were living a Godly lifestyle. And why were we doing all of this talking to other people and not to each other? Because there was division in our home, which is exactly what the devil wanted.

There were times that we were happy. Those were the times when he'd decide to cut everyone off and focus on our family. Then there were times when he'd go off on his selfish tangents. He often went through random spurts like that. Sometimes he was all in and sometimes he wasn't and vice versa. In spite of our emotions, we still had financial problems. Unfortunately, we'd had our electricity cut off more times while we were married than I had when I was single and living alone with my children. The bills weren't getting paid, and he still wanted to spend the money on himself. We had to go stay with my parents several times because he hadn't paid the gas and electric bill. We chose my parents house because he didn't want to go anywhere else. Even in the hardships, we found little spurts of happiness. It was during one of our happy times that we decided to have another baby. We both wanted a girl so we went to the doctor so that I could get off of birth control. We tried for seven months to get pregnant. During the seven months of trying, it became overwhelming raising the boys. So, in the seventh month, we sat down and discussed whether we still wanted another baby at the moment. During the conversation, we decided to wait. So, I set up an appointment with the doctor to get back on birth control. It was at the doctor's office that I found out that I was already pregnant. When I found out, I didn't know whether to be happy or not. In the midst of my confusion, the doctor was more upset than I was. When I got home, I sat down with Drew and told him my news. He was silent for about two minutes straight. After the bout of silence, we both burst out laughing. I mean, what are the odds of me going to the doctor to get on birth control and finding out that I'm already pregnant? It was hilarious. Needless to say, we were both ecstatic. We both really wanted a little girl. And that's exactly what we got.

The first few weeks after finding out that I was pregnant were bliss. He was so kind, loving and attentive. This pregnancy was horrible also so I spent a lot of time sick. It seems like when I started to show, he started to act up again. He would take my car and leave the house at four o'clock in the morning going to work and not return until six o'clock in the evening. He got off of work at ten o'clock in the morning so where was he for all of those hours? I would call him, but he wouldn't answer his cell phone. And I would be stuck in the house sick and alone with the boys. I would often wake up in the middle of the night in the bed alone. I would go downstairs to look for him and he'd be gone. One of those times at around three o'clock in the morning, when I called him, he wasn't answering the phone and when he finally did, he claimed that he'd gotten into a car accident but was on his way home. He didn't come for another two hours. Another time he had taken the car in the middle of the night. When I walked out to get in into the car the next morning, I noticed that there was a dent in a rear upper part of the car on the right-side. When I inquired about it, he told me that it had happened the night of the car accident that supposedly happened.

But it looked more like an angry person kicked my car rather than a car hitting it. This same car that he was stealing, he wouldn't pay the car note on. I had lost my job and was living off of cash assistance from welfare. So, my mother took the car back because it was in her name. I ended up having to use my next tax refund to get another car.

Chapter 10

Divided Before the Fall

It was in my 4th month of pregnancy that I had decided that I couldn't deal with my children alone *and* go through this pregnancy alone. Drew was never home. I was still having problems with not wanting the boys. I wanted my husband and I wanted things to work out. But I was sick, for goodness sakes I was pregnant and I was tired of kids. (Backwards, isn't it?) I needed a break from the boys. So, Drew and I separated. We said that we wanted a divorce, mainly out of anger because neither of us wanted that. He went to stay with his brother and sister-in-law and took the boys with him. Even with all that he was already doing, that was the biggest mistake of my life. I didn't want him to leave, just the boys so that I could rest. After Drew had been gone for three days, he came home with the boys. We sat down and talked. I apologized for everything that I'd done. He apologized for everything he'd done also. I told him that I missed him and asked him to come home and he agreed. For whatever reason, he went back to his brother's that night rather than staying home. It took him about a week to come home. But when he did, he didn't bring all of his stuff. I often asked him when he'd bring it, he'd just reply, "I'll bring it." Soon after, he left again and left me with the boys. He'd often come home and of course we'd have sex, but he never stayed. It was the weekend of our church choir's concert that Drew wanted to keep the boys. I asked him to come to the concert and to bring the boys with him. He said that he was coming, but didn't show up claiming that he had been watching his brother's kids. After the concert, he asked me to come and get him and the boys so I did. He had claimed that his brother and sister-in-law had had car trouble which made him stay later than he had planned. When I picked him up, I saw someone looking out of the window. It was Dogface. Out of suspicion, I asked him who it was. He told me that it was his sister-in-law. They don't favor at all and I know what I saw. He had this chick over here around my children *and* we were still married. And on top of that, I didn't see his brother and sister-in-law's car so that means that they weren't home. I decided to store this information into the back of my mind. After we left there, we went to dinner at Applebee's and went home. We had a lovely and romantic evening. We spent time together. While we were getting ready to get in the shower, he received a telephone call. He left the bathroom, and instantly I felt tension in the atmosphere. When he came back into the bathroom, his demeanor had changed. He was nervous. He came in and said "Bae I need to go back to my brother's house." I asked him why, because we were planning to spend time together. He replied, "I forgot that I have my brother's car keys and he needs them." Well, the car wasn't even there when we left so he couldn't have had the keys. I knew that he was lying, so I asked him to show me the key. He pulled a single house key out of his pocket.

"That's not a car key Drew."

"Yes it is. Look, I have to go." And he took my car and left the house. After waiting up for him for over an hour, I decided to go to bed. Just when I was about to go to sleep, I received a telephone call from his sister-in-law, Gia. I ignored the call and lay down again. She kept calling until I answered the telephone.

"I just thought that you should know that your husband is over here arguing with Dogface."

"Arguing? Arguing about what?"

"She's over here really upset."

"What does she have to be angry about?" I got off

the phone with her and started calling his cell phone. He wouldn't answer though. Gia called me back.

"He's not going to answer the phone."

"Tell him I said to come to the phone."

She started calling his name. As she did, the arguing got louder.

"He's trying to calm her down. I'm telling you, he's not going to leave until she says that she's not mad anymore."

"Who cares if she's mad? That trick is not his wife."

I kept calling him for at least another 20 minutes. I then called my best friend, Ashanti. She was sleep and didn't answer her cell phone. I called the house phone and had her mom wake her up and told her that it was an emergency. She was at my house in like 15 minutes. I had my clothes on so that we could go over there. On our way out of the apartment complex, she ran over a gas can that was lying in the middle of the road. It got stuck under her car and we were afraid to keep moving in case there was gas in the can. She called a friend of hers and he came to help us. Keep in mind that this is the middle of the night, after two o'clock in the morning. While her friend was trying to get the gas can out from under the car, his sister-in-law called me again.

"I know why they were arguing. They've been sleeping together and she's mad that he's with you. I hate to tell you this but y'all are married and this isn't right." Now, mind you, this is the same person that is allowing this chick to sit up in the house all times of the day and night with my husband. She's got some nerve.

"Sleeping together? Since when?"

"They've been sleeping together since October." And this is the month of April. Then Gia starts talking to the trick in the background. "Oh, it only happened once. She was just trying to make you mad."

"What?" I was so upset that I was speechless. As

soon as Ashanti's friend got the gas can out from under the car, we got in the car and got ready to head over to where Drew was. After we moved the car no more than five feet, I saw my car pulling into the complex and some woman was driving it. His brother's car was following it. Then Dogface was following them in her car. The nerve of this whore coming to my house and she's screwing my husband! We turned the car around and went to my apartment. When we did, Dogface turned around and left. I went into the house and Drew was already in there. When I walked in, I saw him grabbing some more of his things. I approached him asking him to explain what was going on. I asked him if he had cheated. His only reply was "it's not like that." I was so pissed off that, yes, I grabbed a knife to try to stab him. As soon as I did, my friend grabbed it. The next thing you know, it got physical. And for whatever reason, his brother had made his way into the house being nosey. I don't know how they ended up leaving, but I was left pregnant and alone. I couldn't stop crying. Ashanti was trying to calm me down. After I calmed down, Ashanti had the nerve to call her mother and her child's father and tell him everything that happened. Did I give her permission to tell my business? I think not!

After that night, my husband and I saw each other often. He kept coming home saying that he'd wanted to stay, but never did. Shortly after, his brother and sister-in-law moved out of town. He came home for a while, but left again claiming to be staying with his brother, a brother that he had hardly talked to over the years. It was on a social media site called Lookout that people were saying that he was living with her. These people would see Drew and Dogface out at Walmart and would post statuses with scriptures on their Lookout page saying:

> "Nevertheless, to avoid fornication, let every man have his own wife, and let every woman have her own husband."
>
> I Corinthians 7:2 KJV

Then after that would put, "God help these Walmart shoppers. That man should be at home with his pregnant wife..." And I later found out that the same people that were posting these statuses were the same ones that told him to leave me in the first place. I was devastated. To embarrass him, when in reality, I was really embarrassing myself I would post things on Lookout too. It was a few days before our first wedding anniversary that all of this was occurring. I posted something similar to this. "It makes no sense that I'll be spending my anniversary alone," amongst other things. I was depressed and fell right into the trap of stupidity. Most people agreed with my posts. But, someone that used to go to my church replied "I'm really sorry that you're going through this. But, you should stop posting all of your business on Lookout (a social media site). Everyone doesn't need to know what's going on in your home." She didn't know, but I was really upset with her because I felt like she didn't know the pain that I was feeling and how could she say that to me when I'm hurting? But her words stuck with me. I didn't listen right away, but eventually I did.

Drew did show up for our anniversary. As usual, since he had been cheating, he wanted to go somewhere out of town so that there was no "drama." We went to dinner in Birch Run, MI and spent the evening in Frankenmuth, MI. These places were at least thirty minutes away from where we lived. I guess there was some significance to it because that's where we went on our first date. There was some huge celebration that was happening there. The evening was beautiful. We were happy, for the night. And we had a good time. His mother had kept the boys for us. The next day, we went to church and then we went to get the boys. That night, he left again. A day later, he came back and stayed a few days. It was a Friday night that our church was having a youth service. I wanted Drew to come with me. He claimed that he needed to get a haircut and to do some other things. He dropped me off at the church and left in my car. Before the service was over, I called him to let him know that I was ready so that I wouldn't be kept waiting. After the service was over, he still hadn't come. While I was waiting outside, I stood around talking to some people from the church. During the conversation, they informed me that our childhood friend had been murdered and the funeral was the next day. I was devastated because he and I had been close when we were younger. I really wanted to go. Pretty much everyone had left the church when Drew finally arrived, and as usual, he hadn't been answering his phone. I was ticked off, again. When we arrived home, I told him about my friend and the funeral and how I really wanted to go. That evening, we spent time together. But, I woke up in bed alone, which was becoming a routine in our marriage. He had left in the middle of the night in my car again. I kept calling him because I really wanted to go to the funeral and I had already gotten dressed.

When he arrived the next day, it was after one

o'clock in the afternoon and the funeral was over. He rushed into the house. I tried to explain to him what he'd done. Instead of listening to me, he hurriedly changed clothes, went downstairs into the kitchen pretending that he was going to stay a while. He grabbed my juice out of the refrigerator. Then he walked to the door and yelled, "Bae I'm going for a jog. I'll be right back," and ran out of the house. I was getting further along in my pregnancy so by the time I got to the door, I saw that he had ran off down the road. When I called him, he kept running. After that day, I didn't see my husband for a month and a half.

As my pregnancy progressed, so did problems with my health. All of the stress in my life was affecting the baby. I ended up going to the doctor numerous times a week. Each time I went, my heart rate was severely high. The doctor began to refer me to specialists and an OBGYN who specialized in high risk pregnancies. Nothing that the doctors did helped. It began to put a major strain on my baby. I tried to tell Drew everything that was happening. By this time, his phone had been disconnected. If there was an emergency, the only way that I could reach him was to email him and wait for him to respond. In the process, Drew's birthday came and a week later mine followed. We had planned to spend our birthdays together. My birthday weekend, my sister told me that she would keep the boys for the weekend. I just had to drive them there, to Lansing. Now, I was seven months pregnant. And I was miserable. On my birthday, the next day, I needed to go grocery shopping for the house but I couldn't stand for long periods of time so I needed help. That morning, Drew called me anonymously to tell me that he was coming. By three o'clock in the afternoon, I decided to get up and go because I knew that he wasn't coming. I did the best that I could. By the time I got to the checkout lane, I was really weak and dizzy and had a hard time standing. But I managed to get it done. By eight o'clock that night, Drew still hadn't showed up. My friend Chelsea had called to check on me. She felt really bad that I'd spent my birthday in the house alone and she invited me over to her mother's house. When I got there, I was still depressed but I felt better because I was around people who cared.

A few days later, Chelsea called to check on me. I was stuck in the house with the boys because the brakes on my car had gone out. I told her that I really hadn't been feeling well. She asked if I'd seen my husband and I told her no. I told her how long it had been since I'd seen him. Chelsea came over to my house and decided that she would help me find him. She picked up me and the boys and we drove over to Dogface's mother's house, which is where I heard that he was staying. I really didn't want any drama. I just wanted to know where my husband was. But I knew how ghetto and dramatic Dogface could be. So, Chelsea got out of the car with me and walked up the stairs with me to knock on the door. It took forever for me to get there because by this time, my stomach was huge. When we knocked on the door, Dogface's sister and mother came to the door. Chelsea asked if Drew was there. Her sister responds, "No, they just left."

I ask, "They, who is they?"

"Drew and Dogface."

"They were here together?" I asked. I didn't know that he would actually be here. I was just curious.

"Yes, they left together."

"Oh, well can you tell him that his wife is looking for him?" I threw it out there just to make sure that they knew they had a married man living in their house.

"Ok, we'll tell him."

When we got to the car, I called Dogface's phone and she didn't answer. By the time we got to the corner, he called back anonymously talking about "You're looking for me?" Well DUH! That's a dumb question. When I asked him where he was so that I could go see him, he lied about where he was so that we couldn't find him. But I could tell by the way he was talking that he left from around her to talk to me. He and I got nothing resolved. After I got off the phone with him, Dogface called back with an attitude with Chelsea and asked Chelsea why she brought me to her house and why we were trying to start drama. Chelsea tried to explain to her that she was sleeping with a married man. And that his wife was seven months pregnant and needed her husband. Dogface doesn't have a lick of sense whatsoever. She went on to say that she didn't care if Drew is married, she had him first. Then she stated that she and Drew were getting married. That's when I cut in to ask how she was going to marry someone who was already married? That made no sense to me. And when she realized how stupid she sounded, she responded, "That's him, ask him." By the time Drew got on the telephone, I was crying. He left from around Dogface again to talk to me. I asked him what she was talking about. He denies saying that he would marry her. (I didn't mention to him that a month or so before, I saw text messages between he and her where she was saying that she had an appointment at David's Bridal.) But then he proceeded to tell me that it was over and that he doesn't want to be with me anymore. I asked him if he was serious. And he repeated it, but it came out like he was having a hard time saying it. I could not believe that he would do this to me. I gave the phone to Chelsea and I got out of the car. As soon as I walked into my house, I started taking down every family photo that he was in. Our wedding photos that we had on the wall, I took them down also. I took everything in sight that reminded me of him and boxed it up. Chelsea walked into the house trying to calm me down, to no avail. After a few minutes, she said "I can't leave you here alone like this. You and the kids are coming with me." We left to go to her apartment. As soon as we got into her house, Drew called. I didn't want to talk to him so I let the phone ring. After his third time calling, I finally answered knowing that he wouldn't stop calling. He asked me how I was doing. Really? What kind of question is that? Then he started apologizing for everything that he did. "I'm really sorry about everything. I didn't mean what I said. I really want our family. She made me tell you that it was over and blah, blah, blah." He then asked if he could come and see me. I told him no. He said that he'll be over in an hour. This is like four o'clock in the afternoon. He didn't show up. Since I knew that he was a habitual liar, Chelsea and I left and went to attend a fun day at Chelsea's daughter's school. I didn't get home until at least nine o'clock. He didn't show up, but he called me doing a lot of begging and apologizing.

The next time I saw Drew was on the day that his brother had watched the kids for me because I had to go to the doctor. His brother was staying with his mom at the time. When I went to get the boys, she told me that she had seen Drew a week ago at a family dinner that I'd missed. It really hurt me because I missed my husband.

And why was it that everyone else had seen him and I hadn't in a month and a half? His mother then told me how on the day of the dinner, his cousin had to go to Dogface's mother's house to convince Drew to come. And that when he did, his grandmother, who isn't alive now, sat him down at the table and talked to him about what he was doing wrong. She told him that he needed to be home with his family and that he couldn't even respond. All he did was sit in the chair and cry. I was upset.

Drew didn't have a phone so I called his mistress and told her to let me speak to my husband. She gave him the telephone and he answered. I asked him where he was and told him to meet me at his mom's. He said that he would be there. An hour later he still hadn't shown up so I called him again. After speaking to him a second time, he finally pulled up in a van that his mistress was driving. I was standing in the driveway of his mother's home watching him try to walk towards me, but Dogface kept calling him and trying to talk to him. I can't describe the pain I felt watching my husband with another woman. And on top of that, I was carrying his child. Drew walked up to me and hugged me like nothing ever happened. Then he started to rub my stomach and talk to the baby.

When Drew and I got into the house, his mother sat both of us down and talked to us. She told him everything that was happening with the baby that I hadn't had a chance to tell him. When she asked him where he wanted to be, at home with his wife and children or with Dogface, he replied that he wanted to be at home with us. She asked him, "So what's the problem? Go home then." After talking for a couple of hours, he decided that he wanted to come home. We went home that night.

The next day I, Drew and the boys went to church with his mom. During altar call, Drew went up for prayer and the evangelist that was praying for him called me up there to pray for the both of us. After church, we went to dinner with his mom. After dinner, we went back to his mom's house. When we walked into the living room, we saw Drew's things sitting in the living room. When we asked where it came from, Drew's brother replied "She (Dogface) brought it over here earlier." I remember his mom saying, "Oh good, she brought his stuff. Now he can go home and not have to be bothered with her again." Drew put his things in the trunk of the car. When we got home, I asked him to bring his stuff into the house. He replied, "I'll do it later." That same day when I got on Lookout, I saw that his family had again posted about us. It was something similar to, "It was good to see my cousin and his wife and children at church today." They did it to upset his mistress.

A few days later, his stuff was still in the trunk of the car. I asked him to bring it in again and he didn't. It was on this day that we were getting ready to take a shower and spend time together. He told me to go on upstairs and that he'd be up after he was done using the bathroom. I waited a few minutes to get into the shower because I had a funny feeling. I went to check on him and he said he'd be right up. I went ahead and got into the shower. When I got out of the shower and got dressed, I walked downstairs to see that he had left again. And on top of that, he had left the door unlocked with me and the children alone in the house with no protection. The next day, his family was having a dinner at his aunt's house and they had invited us. I went with the boys. When I got there, his mom asked where he was. I told them that I didn't know because he had left the night before. His mom asked if he'd taken his stuff. I walked to the trunk of the car to discover that he had. That was another terrible blow to my heart. I was crushed.

My family was aware of all that I was going through. One of my sisters called me and told me that she was concerned about my health and how it was affecting me and my children. She told me that she looked up some Christian counselors in the area. She paid for me to go to four sessions and told me to call and schedule my first appointment. That turned out to be a blessing.

The only counseling that I'd ever been to was marriage counseling at church. I'd never gone to a professional counselor so I didn't know what to expect. It felt a little weird. I didn't have an opportunity to open up like I needed to but, it was nice to talk to someone. When she found out about my situation, she told me that she wanted to bless me and would allow me to continue coming. She asked me to bring my husband. As usual, when I needed him he didn't show up. When I did finally get him to show up, it was one of the last sessions. And he acted like he always does in counseling, acts really serious, like we don't have any problems. Then he says everything that he thinks you want to hear, "I'll do better. I'm going to come home & etc." The next time I saw the counselor, I'd had the baby. I don't remember how we lost touch, but we did.

Chapter 11

Precious Delivery

I went through the rest of the pregnancy alone. I had asked the doctor to tie my tubes. She wouldn't do it because she thought that I felt that way because of all that I had been through. Yes, I had been through a lot. But, I knew that I didn't want anymore kids. I'd planned to have a VBAC (Vaginal Birth after Cesarean). But I scheduled a c-section in case the baby didn't come as soon as I'd liked. The baby didn't come, so we went with the c-section. I told Drew the date that the baby would be born. We had to be at the hospital hours before the surgery. I didn't think that he would show up. He showed up thirty minutes before the time I had to be at the hospital. Even though I was a little uncomfortable, he was very sweet and helpful. We laughed and joked, like normal. Then, when our church family came into the hospital room, tension came too. He felt uncomfortable and started to become introverted out of guilt. Ever since he had started cheating, he always feared that someone would say something to correct him and tell him that he was doing wrong, which they should have. But no one disrespected him. They just told him that they were glad he was there.

When it was almost time for me to go into surgery, the nurse came and asked who was going into the delivery room with me. Both, Drew and my mom raised their hands. The nurse informed them that only one person could go in with me. My mom decided to let him go in, seeing that he was still my husband, and she'd gone in with me when the boys were delivered. I was so afraid. I couldn't stop shaking. It's a blessing that I didn't get hurt when they did the spinal block. While I was on the surgical table, I kept crying because I was really scared. Drew sat next to me and held my hand and comforted me. I didn't feel any pain, but I felt a lot of pressure when they delivered the baby. We were blessed with a little baby girl named Saniyah. When the baby was delivered, she kept hollering and screaming. They wrapped her up in a blanket and handed her to Drew. As soon as he grabbed her, she stopped crying. It was sweet, but it was weird to me because he'd missed most of the pregnancy. Did she really know who he was? Drew held the baby up to me so that I could see her. But a few seconds later, the nurses took the baby for some tests and Drew left me in the operating room alone. I felt abandoned, again. When I returned to my hospital room, a lot of my friends and family were there. It was so funny because I had to ask them to let me see my baby because they were hogging her.

After everyone left, Drew stayed the night with me. The next day, I told him that he could take the car and go home to shower and get dressed. He declined. By the time it was lunchtime, Drew was hungry. He said that he didn't have any money. I gave him my last five dollars so that he could get himself something to eat. He had gone down to the cafeteria with my mother and sister. They didn't know that he didn't have any money. If they had, they would have bought him something to eat.

Because I'd had a c-section, I was in so much pain. I couldn't walk without assistance. The nurses told me that it was okay to take a shower. I couldn't stand on my own for a long period of time so Drew helped me. Later in the evening, we sat together talking and playing with the baby. I began to feel tension in the room. He told me that he was hungry again. I offered him some food, I had plenty of snacks. He said "No thanks. Bae, I'm going to the vending machine. I'll be right back." And he left. I knew that he wasn't coming back. Thirty minutes later I called him to see what he would say. He answered the phone. I could hear from the noise in the background that he was outside. I asked him where he was. He told me that he was on his way to the house to get something that he'd forgotten. I told him that he could've taken the car. He declined. I didn't see him until a day after I got home from the hospital. And the doctor had let me stay two days longer because she knew that I needed the rest. On top of that, he was supposed to have kept the boys while I was still in there.

The day after I got home from the hospital, the baby had a doctor's appointment. Drew's mom drove us because I couldn't drive and my brother had my car. He sat next to me while I filled out the paperwork. When I got to the section where I had to put the names of the parents, I put my name and kept filling out the rest of the paperwork. After I had turned it in and returned to my seat, he said to me, "You know, she has more than one parent."

"Huh?" I replied. I was puzzled.

"You only put down that she has one parent. You didn't put my name down."

"Oh!" I really hadn't realized that I'd done that. But I guess subconsciously, I knew that I would be raising her alone. "I'm sorry. I didn't do it on purpose. You want me to change it?"

He gave me a look as if to say, "You better go change it." But he said "No, you don't have to."

I knew that he wanted me to though. So, I got up and went to the window where my friend, Ashanti worked. I told her that he wants me to put his name on the paper as the baby's parent. She started laughing. I fixed my error and let him see it before I turned it in. He wasn't happy with me. I really didn't do it intentionally, but just as I thought, I was going to be raising Saniyah and our other two children alone.

After we left the doctor, Drew's mother took us to eat before she took us home. After we had been home for a while, Drew left again. There were many nights where I would be up in the middle of the night crying because I was tired. I wasn't getting much sleep because I still had to take care of the boys during the day. That whole, "sleep while the baby sleeps" was non-existent for me because I had two other children to tend to. Drew was still in and out of the house. I had been telling him for years that either he needed to be completely in or completely out of my and my children's lives. But seeing that we were married now, it was hard to tell my husband that he couldn't come home.

About a week after I had the baby, Drew had come home for a day or so. He told me that he had an interview in a city about thirty minutes away and wanted to use my car. Considering the circumstances, I didn't trust him enough to let him take my car. He might not have brought it back. So, the baby and I rode with him. Needless to say, he didn't get the job. And he left us alone, again.

When the baby turned six weeks old, I returned back to church. We got her blessed on that day. (A blessing in our church is when the preacher prays blessings over a child's life. It is also where we vow to provide the child with the opportunity to receive every benefit of the home, the church and the school.) Drew came to church to be a part of the baby's blessing. Many people thought that we were finally happy and had reunited. What they didn't know was that I had gotten all of the kids dressed by myself and I was exhausted. By this time, I didn't even want to go. I was unhappy, I wanted my family back and I wanted my life to be different.

When I finally got to the church, Drew was in the parking lot waiting for me and we walked in together. He beat me there because Dogface's mother's house (where he was still staying) was down the street from the church. Drew's mom and sister came to church to be a part of the blessing. That was good because his family rarely came to our family functions.

After church, Drew's mom took us all out to dinner. Of course, she tried to encourage him to do the right thing and move back in with his family. He didn't stay though. He returned the next Saturday night to go to church with me. When people saw him, I guess they assumed that we were working it out. In the middle of that week when I came home, I found a note on my door from the leasing office saying, "We notice that you have another person living in your home and you need to come and add them to the lease." I called them to see what they were talking about because I had told them about the baby. When I spoke to the manager, I asked what they were referring to.

She said "I'm talking about your husband."

"He doesn't live with me."

"Oh really? Well we have people that have been

seeing him there."

"Well how have they been seeing him when I barely see him myself?" After that, the leasing office left me alone. I know who told them this information. This person attended our church and just assumed that we were living together because they saw him at church. This goes to show you that things aren't always as though they appear. It was bad enough that I was going through this. But to have people causing unnecessary stress was like adding insult to injury.

Drew wasn't getting any better. Each time he'd come home, Dogface would have someone call to start drama. One day, she had her friend call my phone looking for him. He had me lying for him saying that he wasn't with me. The girl had the nerve to say to me, "I'm sick of this. Tell him that he needs to make up his mind whether he wants to be with you or her." Was this girl crazy? He has a wife and three kids. Who is he supposed to be with?

There were times when Dogface would inbox me

on Lookout, and other times she would post things on his Lookout page. One of the times she inboxed me, it read "Tell that bitch ass nigga that he could have faced me like a man. He left when I was sleep and I know he's with you because the boys' bag is gone." (I saved this message in case I wanted to use it in court later. But Drew eventually hacked into my account and deleted it.) This happened during one of the times that he had called me around four o'clock in the morning saying that he wanted to come home, and he came. He also had gone to church with me and the kids. I showed him the message. He told me not to respond to it, so I didn't.

Later that evening, after the boys had gone to bed, Drew and I sat down and talked. While we were talking, I received a text message saying "That fat girl is posting things on Drew's page. You might want to look at it." I didn't look at it though. I just had them tell me what it said. She was asking him where he is, saying that she's looking for him and that he needs to hurry up and come home. I just couldn't understand how I ended up in this mess. Since when is it wrong for a man to be at home with his wife and children? That night, I tried to get a deeper understanding of why he was doing this. I asked him why he wouldn't just come home. This night was the first time he actually offered some type of explanation. He said to me that he didn't want to come home because it was safer for me and the children if he stayed away, and that he didn't want anything to happen to us. I asked him why he felt that something would happen to us and he told me that she would try to hurt him. After I asked this question, he logged onto Lookout and read to me a message that she'd sent to his inbox. "If you don't come home right now I'm going to bleach all of your clothes and you gone need the police to save you." She also stated other things that I choose not to share. After he read the message, he left, saying that he would take care of it and would be back that night. He didn't come back. I didn't see the message myself and I don't know if he was telling me the truth about what she'd sent him, but

I'd known from previous experiences that this girl was crazy, so you never knew with her.

Our baby was seven months old when Drew actually bought her something, other than when he bought her something at the beginning of the pregnancy. Back then, he bought a rocking chair, for me, and a box of diapers for the baby. I was having a hard time providing for the children, and they all needed things. He bought the baby a pack of diapers, a can of formula, baby wipes and an outfit. I must say that if it hadn't been for Drew's mom, my baby wouldn't have had anything. While I was pregnant, all I had been able to buy her was a crib, car seat, stroller, some t-shirts, and socks. She didn't have anything. His mom bought her a high chair and clothes. The rest of the things she had had come from the baby shower, which he hadn't shown up to. The baby was growing really fast too. Every time the baby needed something, his mother got it for her. After a while, she got tired because he wasn't doing anything. My mom didn't do anything because she figured that if she didn't, he would step up. Well…he didn't.

Chapter 12

Weary and Wounded

During this entire situation, I prayed often. I read my bible every day, all day. I was tired of being married and still single. And most importantly, I was tired of sharing my husband. I know now that I shouldn't have kept sleeping with him. At the time, I didn't see it like that. I was just looking at the fact that I had needs and it is permissible in marriage to fulfill those needs, which is normal; although there was nothing normal about our marriage at all.

When Drew had started cheating, I felt it in our

bedroom first, and then I found out in other ways. I could literally feel other women in our bed. It's an indescribable feeling, but to try to put it into words, I could feel a lot of different spirits that didn't belong there. While doing this, I felt dirty. Sleeping with my husband went from being an awesome experience to something short of torture. It had gotten to the point where it felt like sleeping with him was no longer sacred, but was a sin. I actually called my Pastor, Pastor Austin, and asked him if it was. He assured me that it wasn't, but his assurance didn't change the way that it felt.

At first, Drew was the gentlest, kind and sweetest person that I knew. He respected me, and my body. He never forced me to do anything that I didn't want to do. If he wanted it, he would wait to see if I did before pursuing me. Somewhere along the way, that all changed. There was a shift in his mind. It's like he went from being mentally normal to being controlled by something evil. He became different, dark. There would be times when he'd forget who he was in bed with. Now, I liked to try new things but he became perverted and disrespectful. I would often think, "Oh, that's what he does to her, huh? And she actually let him?" I would wake up in the middle of the night to him trying to have sex with me and by the time I was fully woke; he already was having sex with me. He didn't consider whether I wanted to or not. My feelings and desires became a non-factor. His care for me became non-existent. And when I tried to express it to him, he didn't understand what I meant. Well, it was either that he really didn't understand, or he no longer cared.

I was growing weary in our marriage. While I was pregnant and after I'd had the baby, I had been searching the scriptures to see what God's plan for marriage was. I knew that when God created marriage, His intent was for it to last forever. He allowed Moses to permit the Pharisees to write a certificate of divorce because of the hardness of their hearts (Mark 10: 2-5 NIV). I studied every scripture in the bible regarding marriage, adultery and divorce. I didn't want a divorce, but my husband wouldn't come home and stay home. He had come home and left over thirteen times. After the thirteenth time, I stopped keeping track. I couldn't go on living this way and I needed to know that if I divorced my husband, I would be okay to marry again since I remained faithful to him and our marriage. I was also concerned that maybe divorce was a sin considering we vowed to be together "for better or worse, richer or poorer, through sickness and health, till death do we part." Since I vowed until death, am I wrong for divorcing him considering that he abandoned me and our children to go live with another woman?

After he had been gone for close to a year, I filed for divorce. I was afraid to file, and I was afraid to serve him with the papers. I was unsure of how he'd react. I had become accustomed to being manipulated by him. What would he do if he feels that his control over me was being threatened? Despite what he was doing to me, I didn't want to hurt him and I still loved him and I didn't really want to get a divorce. In my mind, I honestly thought that if he saw that I was serious about ending our marriage, he would get his act together and come home so that we could work it out. After I filed the papers, the court made us wait six months for our court date. This is customary in Michigan when you have children. The six months is supposed to give you time to work things out and cancel the divorce proceedings.

I was afraid to serve Drew the divorce papers while we were alone so I called Pastor Austin and told him the situation. I asked if it was okay for us to come to the church like we're expecting to have a counseling session, he agreed. When we got there, Pastor Austin asked for updates on our situation and if Drew had come home yet. Of course, the answer was no. He talked for a few minutes and then gave me the go ahead to speak. I was so nervous that I wanted to cry. I told Drew the real reason why I called him there. I explained to him that I'd done everything I knew to do to make our marriage work and that my efforts have been unsuccessful. I told him that I'd filed for a divorce. I made sure to explain to him that I didn't want a divorce, but that I would no longer share my husband with another woman. I handed Drew the divorce papers and then told him that if he wanted to come home, then we could forget about the divorce and move forward with our lives. When I handed him the papers, he started crying and wouldn't even look at me. Pastor Austin asked him how he felt about what I'd said. Drew said that he understood what I was saying.

"Okay, you understand but how do you feel about it?" asked Pastor Austin.

"I mean, I don't like it."

"Let me ask you this, do you feel like you can't be faithful to your wife?"

"Yes, I can be faithful."

"Well, why do you cheat?"

"I don't know."

"What is it? Is it something you're not satisfied with? Is it s.." He stops talking and looks at me, and says "Do you mind leaving the room for a minute?"

"No, I don't mind," I reply. And I get up to leave. I have the baby with me so this gives me a chance to change her diaper. I'm glad that he asked me to leave the room because I know exactly what he is about to get into. About fifteen minutes later, Drew comes down to get me. When I walk back into the room, it is extremely silent. And the tension that is in the room is really thick.

Pastor Austin pauses before he speaks again. "Go home son. Just go home." Drew replies that he will. And he did, but then he left again.

I prayed every day. I continuously asked God what He wanted me to do. He didn't give me an answer though. I later learned that when you're asking God for an answer and He keeps silent, that means to wait. While I was waiting, I was left alone. I didn't have anyone to talk to. No one cared and if they did care, they didn't understand. When I filed the papers, it was a week after Thanksgiving. Our daughter was a little over two months old. Even though our baby was too young to know it, Drew had missed her first Thanksgiving and Christmas. And he hadn't even bothered to call. How could a man not be with his wife and children during the holidays, but be with his mistress and her family, even if they are having problems in their marriage? On Christmas, Drew's mom had invited us over for a family dinner. His aunt was hosting it. I went over there with my children, and Drew's family was expecting to see him with us. They asked me if I had talked to him and I told them that I hadn't. I was hurt, angry and humiliated all at once.

A few months later, in February, I had just started a

new job. It was only a temporary position, but for the first time ever, I could actually pay my bills and get my children everything that they needed. While I was at work, Drew called me to tell me that a local pastor, Pastor Kelly, had reached out to him on Lookout. He told me that they'd been talking for a few weeks and that Pastor Kelly had been encouraging him and wanted us to come in for a counseling session. By this time, I was feeling like I didn't care and I really didn't want to be bothered. When Drew had first asked me to go to counseling, I told him no. Later, I asked him, "What's the purpose in going?"

He replied, "I really want to work out our marriage. I think that this will help us."

I didn't want to go but I felt like I would be contributing to the problem if I didn't at least try. So, I started to ask questions. "Well, when is the appointment?"

"I have an appointment scheduled for today. Will

you please come? He really wants to meet you."

"Today? Are you serious?"

"I know it's last minute, but please come."

Even though I didn't want to go, I went with him. I knew the Pastor from his affiliation with my previous church so I was somewhat familiar with him. When we got there, we told him what was going on. I told him that I had filed for a divorce. He inquired about how many months we had until the divorce would be final, which was four months. After listening, Pastor Kelly told us some things that he wanted to do to help us. Before he went into detail, he gave us paperwork that we needed to complete along with an informal contract. Then he went on to discuss a few ground rules. The contract stated that this was to be taken seriously and that we needed to do everything that he asked us to do for our marriage to succeed. He gave us homework assignments. He then reiterated that "being lazy was not acceptable. Homework assignments need to be completed at home.

You can't come to your session and then be racing trying to finish it in the lobby. If I find that you're not doing the work, then the counseling sessions will cease." He made sure that we both understood. Before we left the counseling session, Drew scheduled another session for the next week. After leaving, we discussed the session in the car. Even though I hadn't wanted to go, on the inside I was excited. Drew was excited too. We needed a change and this might be the help that we were looking for. Drew went home with me and the children that night, but he left again. He claimed that he was going to end it with her and needed to go and get his things.

A week later, I'd completed my homework assignment. What I loved about counseling with this pastor was that he didn't just stay on the surface of things. The homework that he gave us was a series of tests that would tell him things we had been through in our past. It would tell him if we were depressed, mentally unstable, and even what our love languages are (how we communicate love, and desire for it to be communicated with us). I hadn't seen Drew since the last time we'd had counseling. When he arrived, he hadn't completed his homework; typical Drew. Pastor Kelly was lenient this time because he allowed Drew to turn it in the next session.

After starting counseling, things still didn't change. On maybe our third session, Pastor Kelly sent us home with another homework assignment that had to be completed that night. We had to go into the kitchen and pop popcorn, homemade. We had to use popcorn kernels, and even melt our own butter. We were expected to do everything together and the both of us had to stay in the kitchen until the process was done. After popping the popcorn, we were to watch the movie "Fireproof" together. We had already had the movie because my sister gave us the movie for our first Christmas as husband and wife. We survived popping the popcorn. Neither of us knew what we were doing and it was hilarious. During the movie, Drew seemed distracted. He wasn't really into the movie. After the movie and getting what he wanted (sex), he left claiming that he was late for work and had to leave.

Drew had scheduled our next counseling session. He said that he was going to meet me there. When I got there, he didn't show up. I ended up going into counseling by myself. I felt weird because this was supposed to be marriage counseling. It made no sense to be in marriage counseling alone. But, I must say that talking to Pastor Kelly really helped me and it changed my life. I cried the entire session. I knew that I was hurting, but I hadn't known to what extent and this was the first time that I'd ever told anyone what I was really feeling. I scheduled the next session for the both of us, but I was the only one that showed up to the next one. Before I left, Pastor Kelly gave me a workbook for anger. I started it but didn't finish it because doing the assignments in the workbook just made me angrier.

One thing that bothered me most was that Drew was the one that scheduled the counseling sessions in the first place, but after the sessions, he would go back with his mistress. How could we practice what we had learned in counseling if he wasn't at home with me? If he was just going to stay with her, then starting counseling in the first place was pointless. On top of not showing up to counseling, he was never there for me and our children. I was really starting to get angrier and more frustrated. Plus, I had just had a baby so my emotions were all over the place. I started to think of things that I could do to get my husband back and to make our marriage work. In thinking, I concluded that the only way that he will come home is if he has no one else to live with. It was weird to me that before we got married, he didn't have a place to stay and there was no one else that he could stay with. But after we were married, he had everyone in the world to stay with. I know that he's a liar and there's no telling what he may have told these people. But at the end of the day, this was a married man. No matter what he said, everyone that he approached should have said no and sent him home.

Chapter 13

Something Brewing

At this point, I hated Dogface. This was the first time that I had ever hated anyone in my life, and I didn't like the way that it felt. I had never liked her anyway because she'd always been a problem, but ruining my marriage was crossing the line. And not just that, the bible clearly states, "What God has joined together, let no one separate" (Mark 10:9 NIV). Yes, both of them were wrong and he's the one that committed his life to me, but I wanted her out of the picture…permanently.

I began to think of ways that I could seek revenge on her. At first it just started with me wanting to hurt her. I just wanted to teach her a lesson. Over time, that wasn't enough. I wanted her completely out of the picture. I had prayed ever since I'd found out that my husband was cheating for God to move her out of the way, to help him see clearly that he was doing wrong, and to restore my marriage. Even after praying, this girl just would not leave. And for her to blatantly say that she doesn't care that he's married and that she had him first? I wanted her gone so I started planning to kill her.

At first, I wanted to stab her a few times. Over time, that just didn't seem to be enough. So, I decided that I would just shoot her in the head. Well, that would be quick and painless. My children and I have suffered so I wanted her to suffer like we did. That's when I came up with the idea to torture her. I began to think of all the times that she'd called my telephone and harassed me, then all the times that she came to my house acting delirious. On top of that, I had suffered through my entire pregnancy alone while she was laid up with my husband. Then I thought of every time my children cried, had tantrums, and disrespected me because they wanted their dad at home, and I cried even more than them. There was also the fact that our daughter didn't start getting to know her father until she was one year old. And now, my children don't have a father at all. I was supposed to spend the rest of my life with my husband. The vows that we made ensured that I shouldn't have to share my husband with another woman. These thoughts ran rampant in my mind. I hated her and I wanted her gone. Yeah, that's it. I'm going to torture her, then shoot her and set her on fire. At this point, I was feeling as though I'd lost everything I had already. I didn't have anything else to lose. My children don't have a father, but my mother can raise them while I'm in jail, that's if I get caught. My mind was definitely under attack. I didn't realize it, but if I had killed Dogface, I probably wouldn't have cared. I knew what I wanted to do. I just had to implement a plan.

One day Drew called me around six o'clock in the morning while I was up getting ready for work. He asked me if I slept okay. I told him yes and asked why. He replied, "My cousin got murdered last night. Go look out of the window." She wasn't actually related to Drew. She had a baby with his cousin, and she lived in the building next to mine. I went to look out of the window to see a lot of police cars, police tape, and the arson investigator. She had been stabbed. Her daughter was hurt. And the murderer had set the apartment on fire. Seeing that scene was a horrendous experience and I was terrified for months. Drew was the one that had told me about it so he had known before I did. He knew that I was afraid, and that I was in the home alone with our children. Yet, he only came by once. And it wasn't to check on us. He wanted sex from me.

It was when I viewed her body at the funeral home that I began to feel guilty. What was done to her was almost the same thing that I had planned to do to Dogface. I didn't go to the funeral but Drew went, with Dogface. I was still angry, and worried. I knew that what I was feeling wasn't healthy. I called Pastor Austin to discuss how I was feeling and my plans. At the end of the conversation, I was beginning to have a change of heart. I just needed to be reminded that regardless of my circumstances, I still have value. And I have my children to live for, whether my husband returns home or not.

When it got closer to the date of our divorce hearing, Drew started coming to our counseling sessions again. In this session, we'd brought all three of our children along with us. I wanted to see if we could figure out a way to talk to the children to see how they would feel about their mom and dad divorcing. They were too young to express themselves so we were unsuccessful. After talking to Pastor Kelly for a few minutes, he asked us to leave the room so that he could talk to Drew alone.

I don't know what they discussed while they were in the room because Drew never told me. He had no problem telling me anything else, but anytime someone corrected him or put him in his place, he never wanted to share it with me. Maybe he did it out of guilt? I did find out later that Pastor Kelly wanted to talk to Drew about what was going on within. At this point, he was so unhappy but acted as though he didn't know what to do to change it. He knew the right thing to do, but did not do it, either because he didn't know how, or maybe he didn't want to.

I was at my wits end. I was having a hard time accepting what was about to happen. With all my heart, I really wanted things to change. I had done everything that I could. I was having a hard time understanding that I couldn't change him, nor could I change the situation. I fought, and fought, until I couldn't fight anymore. It was time to start accepting it. Just the mere thought of having to accept this made me furious. I was hurt and very angry. I knew who to blame but couldn't take my frustrations out on anyone. I didn't have an outlet. And I rarely had a break from the children, which maximized my frustrations. I wanted to hit someone so bad. I was afraid of what my anger would do to my children so I looked into boxing at the Berston Field House. The class didn't cost much, but I couldn't afford it. When I did finally come up with the money, I didn't have anyone to watch the children. The class would have only lasted about two hours daily. But I still couldn't get anyone to watch them. With practically no support, I was forced to keep my emotions and true feelings internally. A fire will only stay contained for so long before it spreads and destroys everything. And a fire is exactly what was brewing on the inside of me.

This entire experience made me humbler than I'd ever been before. I was beginning to lose myself. I had no one to turn to so I was forced to turn to God. I prayed every step of the way for direction. When I didn't listen, my life became more and more complicated. I began to read a lot of inspirational books. Anyone that knows me knows that I am an avid reader. But until I had started going through this, I'd never completed an inspirational book. I purchased "The Five Love Languages," "Desperate Marriages," and "Hope for the Separated," all by Gary Chapman. When I got into "Desperate Marriages" and "Hope for the Separated," I ended up stopping because I began to see that I wasn't the one with the problem. With the help of God, I had changed myself so now all there was left to do was depend on God. This is an extremely hard thing to do. My mind and emotions began to shift in and out of grief. I didn't know it at the time, but there are five stages of grief. The stages are Denial, Anger, Bargaining, Depression, and Acceptance (Wikipedia).

Even though I knew that my husband was no longer living with me and our children, I still had a hard time accepting it; Denial. Although he was the one that left and was cheating, he was in denial also. The entire time that he was gone and even after the divorce he was still telling people that we were married. This was weird because people were seeing him all over town with this girl. So, he actually thought that it was okay to be with her and he has a wife? Many times, when people saw him with her they would ask, "Where's your wife? How's your wife doing?" He would reply, "Oh, she's at home." Or he would say whatever he came up with at the time. The sad part was that he never really knew where I was or how I was doing for that matter.

Not only was I upset, I was depressed. I wanted my husband to come home because I loved him. I was also hurt because when he came into my life, things went downhill. I had children when I'd never intended to and he left me. Who brings children into the world and walks out on them? He wouldn't even talk to them. When we had the children, we both agreed that it was best for our children to be raised in a two-parent home with BOTH of their parents. I felt like I couldn't handle raising three children alone. Then there were times when I flat out didn't want to. He would call and say that he wanted to be home. And sometimes I would be so emotional that I would call him and ask him to come home. He told me that he felt like it was unsafe to be with me because of her. He was also uncomfortable because of how he humiliated me. So, I began to bargain with him. When he came home, we would visit other churches because he didn't want to go to ours. He said that he didn't feel like dealing with anyone, which meant to me that he was embarrassed. I told him that I loved him and that we could get through this situation together. I told him that I would be with him every step of the way. And I was. If he wanted to move out of Michigan, we could. If he wanted to go to another church permanently, we could. If it meant that we could be together, honor our vows and raise our children together, then I would do it. Now tell me, why was I willing to give up so much when I wasn't the one that had done anything wrong? It was because through this experience, God taught me how to love with an unconditional and unselfish love. Some people thought that it wasn't necessary to make these kinds of sacrifices. But when you're married you're not just your own person anymore. You're connected with someone and you become accountable to and for them. So, moving meant that we could have a fresh start to focus on God, our marriage and our children without the negative outside influences that we had.

Since my emotions were all over the place, there were also times when I was excited about the divorce. These were the times when I was happy because I wouldn't have to share my husband anymore. People would tell me "If he wants to leave, let him." I thought that this was the dumbest statement because I would be letting this whore have my husband. I felt like I should fight, which I did. But in retrospect, if he didn't love God enough to honor our vows and respect me, was he really worth having? I also felt like I had suffered for well over a year and that when the divorce was over, I would be happy and everything would be fine. Boy, was I wrong.

Chapter 14

Moment of Truth

The court date for the divorce was approaching quickly. A week before our court date was scheduled we went to a counseling session with Pastor Kelly. I am extremely thankful for him because he really believed in our marriage and wanted to help us. The session was to ensure that the both of us really wanted this divorce and to see if there was anything else that we could do to prevent it, because neither of us actually wanted it. My first attempts at getting the divorce were blocked by Drew. I didn't have money for an attorney so I had to do the entire process by myself. I went to a company that provides free legal services to people that can't afford it to see if they would help me. When I got there, they wouldn't help me because they said that he was a client in the same matter. No papers had been filed so how was he a client? When I asked Drew about it, he swore that he'd only gone to get information from them. In reality, he'd really gone down there and talked to them to try to stop me from getting the divorce. I couldn't understand why he would try to stop me from getting a divorce and he wouldn't come home. Although in the counseling session he stated that he didn't want the divorce, he hadn't done anything to prove it. And most importantly, he hadn't changed his actions. In other words, he wanted to do what he wanted but still have me at home waiting for him.

The next week we went to court for the divorce hearing. I was so afraid. I got there before Drew did and even while waiting, I still didn't want to go through it.

When I saw him, my heart started racing. But my heart wasn't racing just out of fear. I was still in love with my husband. We weren't allowed to take cell phones into the building so he'd ditched his in a bush. When he came in, he asked if he could put his phone in my car. I gave him the keys and told him where the car was parked. When he came back, we sat outside of the courtroom in silence. There were a lot of empty chairs in the room and he chose to sit right next to me. My mind was already frazzled but the smell of his cologne didn't help matters at all. Then he attempted to hold a conversation with me like we were just casually waiting to be seated in a restaurant or something. I felt bad that we were there and I was uncomfortable. When we got into the hearing, the referee looked over the papers and asked a few questions for clarification of what I was requesting from the court. I'd made a few errors on the forms. A few she let me correct. But I needed proof for one of the items on the forms so the referee told me to get everything in order and that we were adjourned until the same time next week.

When we left the courtroom, Drew was super nice. I ended up taking him to the bus station so that he could go home. So, as we walked to my car together, he held a conversation with me. When we got to the car he opened my car door, like he used to do before he had started cheating. He seemed nice, but it didn't seem sincere. It was like he had a reason for being nice. Before he left, he asked again the date and time of the next court date and I told him. A few days later Drew called me to ask me about the court date again. He wanted to clarify the date and time. I told him. While we were on the telephone, he asked me if I was sure that I wanted to go through with the divorce. Instead of answering him, I asked him if he was going to change. He said that he would, yet he didn't.

The date of the hearing came. He called me all morning to see if I was still going, to see the time of the hearing, and to say that he would meet me there.

When I got there, I checked in with the clerk and waited. I moved to the other waiting area and waited some more. After about an hour, the referee called me back and Drew still hadn't shown up. When I got into the courtroom, before we went "on the record," the referee asked me if I'd gotten everything together. I told her that I believed I had and gave her the papers. When we went "on the record," the referee asked me to state my name and the correct spelling of it. She went on to state that the defendant, Drew wasn't present. She asked me what the breakdown in our marriage had been and why I'm here today seeking a divorce. I stated that "my husband left me and our children to go live with another woman." She said, "Wow, well there has been a breakdown." The referee granted the divorce and told me to go and get it signed by the attorney and turn it in. When I got to the attorney's office, I waited in line. While I waited, I still had some hesitation. After getting the papers signed by the attorney's office, I sat down on a bench a few feet from the office. When I'd first sat down, it was to make sure that I had all my papers organized and that I knew what I needed to do next. After doing so, I sat for about thirty minutes and contemplated what I was going to do. I reasoned with myself about whether I was doing the right thing. I knew that my husband hadn't changed, but I still loved him. Eventually, I told myself that if I didn't do it today, then I never would and if I didn't take a stand, he was going to forever run over me and do what he wanted to me anyway. I took the long walk to the elevator and ascended to the next floor. I waited in line. When it was my turn, the clerk looked over the papers and processed them. I asked her if there was anything else I needed to do. She told me no and that when the divorce is final, it will be in the newspaper and that I was all set.

When I left the courthouse, and had gotten into my car, I noticed that I had a lot of missed calls from Drew. I called him back and asked him why he hadn't shown up. He told me that he didn't have a ride. He didn't have a ride? He rode the bus to the first hearing. He couldn't have done the same thing this time? When I'd asked him this, he claimed that he didn't have the money. How could he not have $1.35? He got money from Dogface all the time, I'm sure he could have gotten that from her too. Not only that, he kept a bus pass so I'm sure he had one of those too.

Drew went on to ask me what happened in court. I told him that the referee granted the divorce and he was not happy with me. He went on to ask me why I filed for the divorce and how he'd never wanted it and went on and on trying to make me feel bad. I already felt bad and regretted my decision. He was the cause of all of this and now he had the nerve to make me feel bad about divorcing him when he was cheating on me with other women (I had later found out that it was more than one woman). And to make matters worse, he still hadn't changed.

Chapter 15

Changing Hearts

A few weeks after I turned the divorce papers in to the clerk, I decided to follow the court order and allow Drew to get the children every other weekend. This was hard for me to do considering the circumstances. He was still living with Dogface and was lying about it. I didn't want my children around the two of them considering what they had done to our marriage. And on top of that, Dogface was crazy and neither she or Drew could be trusted.

The first weekend that I let Drew get the children

was extremely difficult because it was my birthday weekend. That weekend, my dad had gone into the hospital after having a seizure and a major heart attack. I was lost without my children because I never got a break and didn't know what to do with myself. And on top of that, no one in my family wanted to at least go to dinner with me for my birthday. I was depressed because for the last seven and a half years, Drew and I had spent all holidays together, major and minor. I ended up going to dinner with some people from my church. It was nice to get out of the house but I don't think I did a good job of masking my feelings.

Allowing my children to go with Drew for the weekends was a big mistake, on my part. And it turned into a heart-wrenching experience. He would tell me that he was staying with his mom or his god mom, and that's where I would meet him to drop the kids off. He would call me every couple of hours from his mom's house to let me know that he was there. But he would leave and go back around the corner to where he was staying with Dogface at her mother's house. Allowing Drew to get my children, to me, went against everything that I believed and everything that we had discussed as far as what we wanted for our children. We'd both wanted our children to be raised with both of their parents in the home. I wanted it because I was raised with my parents being married and they were both in the home. He wanted it because he'd never had it and when he was younger he'd always said that that's what he would give his children, when he had some. Seeing that this is what we'd both planned for, neither of us were proactive by taking precautions and thinking of the possibility of us not being together forever. I guess we'd honestly felt that we would spend the rest of our lives together. Clearly, that was not the case.

The divorce caused a lot of problems in my home. It created a tension that was extremely thick. I was missing my husband and my children were missing their father. Well, Saniyah didn't really know him and she still doesn't to this day. My boys were so unhappy that they constantly began to disrespect me. They were so hard-headed and I couldn't get them to obey me, no matter what I did. I'm sure they felt like I was to blame for their dad not being with us anymore. They were too young to express themselves and I'm sure that sometimes they felt like it was their fault. I spent a lot of time re-building our relationships and then they would go with Drew on his weekend. When they would get home, I would have to put in double time trying to get things back to where they were before they left. This was exhausting and to me, it was not needed seeing that I was raising three children alone. But I told myself that he was their father and even though I'd been telling him for years that he can't keep coming in and out of their lives, I allowed him to anyway. Now, because the court ordered me to, I was allowing my children to go into a very messy situation because I felt that if I didn't let them go, I would be penalized in some type of way. I also knew how much they missed their dad and I wanted my children to have a father. At the time, I thought that I was handling the situation correctly, but truthfully, I wasn't.

On top of all of this, I was having a hard time grasping the fact that he and I were no longer married. I was nowhere near accepting it. I had been with Drew for seven and a half years. He was the only person that I'd slept with since before we were married, and even after the divorce, we were still sleeping together. I didn't realize it at the time but this was contributing to the problem.

Drew got the children on his weekends for a few months. Then, as usual, he stopped getting them. Again, my children had to readjust to not being with their dad on a regular basis. He would still come by, but that was for sex. And because I wanted it too, I gave it to him. This cycle didn't stop until I began to realize how it was destroying me spiritually and mentally. And it was also creating a harmful dynamic in my household. I was being stupid, but thought that I had control of the situation and that what I was doing wasn't doing any harm to me.

After a few months, I was back in counseling with Pastor Kelly. I was having a hard time forgiving Drew for everything he'd done to me. And even worse, I hadn't forgiven myself for the part that I'd played in it also. I hated myself for allowing him to ruin my life. I hated myself for letting him convince me to have children that neither of us wanted. I hadn't forgiven myself because ever since he'd been in my life, my life had gone downhill and I ended up being stuck in poverty. I hadn't forgiven either of us and I didn't understand how to forgive someone when the situation was still relevant. How could I forgive him and he hadn't changed and was still with the woman that he'd left me for?

Drew decided that he wanted to start getting the children again and because I hadn't forgiven him, I didn't want him to. But since I was sincerely seeking to be set free, I did everything that Pastor Kelly asked me to do. What's the point in going to counseling if you're not going to take the counselor's advice? I felt that in exchange for him giving me his time, I had to at least try what he was asking of me and put it into action. Pastor Kelly suggested that I call or write Drew a letter and set up a meeting with him and his girlfriend so that we could openly discuss what I expected as far as my children. I talked with Pastor Kelly's wife to think of a neutral location where we could meet. We decided on a park in Grand Blanc, MI. After the appointment was set on the calendar, I emailed Drew asking if they would meet me and Pastor Kelly. I surprised myself by being extremely nice when I really wanted to hurt the both of them. This is what I wrote:

Hi Drew,

I'm writing to see if I could meet with you and your girlfriend. I feel that it's time that we come to an agreement, and some type of understanding about our children and how we intend to care for, and provide for them…seeing that you and I are no longer married.

There will be a mediator, Pastor Kelly. We will meet in a neutral place, at Physicians Park in Grand Blanc. The date is Tuesday, June 19 at 4p. The address is 218 Church St, near the Tim Horton's on Saginaw Rd.

Please let me know if this day and time will work for you.

Cassandra

P.S. You may feel that there's no reason for her to be there. But, since that's who you're with and you intend to have her around our children, I feel that it's important for her to be there also.

Drew didn't respond to the email. I talked to him the day of the meeting on instant messenger. He said that he was coming but, like I thought, he wanted to know why she needed to be there. He knew that neither I nor she liked each other. And for all of the time that he'd been gone, he'd worked overtime to keep us away from each other because he didn't want either of us to "put him on blast" about the things he'd been doing, and was still doing. I told him that she needed to be there because he'd been sneaking and having her around my children even though he knew that I didn't want that. I told him that since he's just going to do it anyway, I need to talk to her directly so that there's no confusion about my expectations.

I arrived at the park at approximately 3:45pm. I was there before anyone else. Pastor Kelly arrived next. We chose a spot to sit at and discussed what we expected out of the meeting before they arrived. About five minutes into waiting, Drew called and asked for directions. After Pastor Kelly gave Drew the directions, he asked me if I thought that Dogface was with him. I had heard her in the background so I knew that she was. I had to mentally prepare myself because I really hated this girl.

The minute I saw her with Drew, my blood started to boil. Granted, he wasn't my husband anymore, but in my heart he was. And I didn't want to see him with another woman, especially someone who is a downgrade from me. This girl is extremely fat and ugly. When I call her Dogface, I do it because that's really what she looks like. On top of that, she's really ugly personality-wise, and also ugly as far as respect, morals and values. There have been plenty of times when my mom saw them at the mall or someplace else and she always commented on how much bigger and taller she was than him. My mom would always say that Dogface looked as if she was his mother and he that tagged behind her like a little boy. When they arrived, that's exactly what I saw. He was walking a few feet behind her. And when she stood next to him, it was uneven. Even while noticing that, I'd wished that I had brought a gun so that I could shoot her in the face. Then she had the nerve to sit directly across from me. He sat on the same side as her, but made sure to scoot away from her…guilt.

When they sat down, Pastor Kelly said a prayer and gave them a brief introduction to why we were there today. He only spoke for about 3 minutes and then he left the rest up to me. I'd written down some things that I wanted to say. But I still felt unprepared. I'm sure that it was because of the circumstances. I thanked them for coming...Wow! That was true growth right there. I went on to reiterate why we were there. The first thing that I discussed was my concern for the safety of my children. I explained that I was apprehensive about even letting the two of them get my children because of the lifestyle that he was living. I looked directly at Drew and told him that I had heard about some of the things that he had been doing and that it concerned me because if someone were to retaliate against him, I didn't want my children to get hurt in the cross fire. I made sure that he understood that he was to protect my children at all costs. While I was talking, Dogface cut in saying, "Stuff? What is this stuff that he's doing?" I looked at her and told her, "If you want to know, ask him." After she did, Pastor Kelly cut in reminding us to stay on the topic of why we were there.

My concern came from all of the women that he was sleeping with. Drew had been messing with a married woman for some time, in addition to Dogface and some other women. I don't know if the woman's husband knew about it, but I do know that some people will actually murder someone if they find out that their spouse is cheating. I know this because I wanted to commit a murder myself. And it's truly by the grace of God that I didn't.

I went over the schedule that was given to us by the court and made sure that they understood that they were to have the children every other weekend and that we were to alternate holidays. The day of pick-up was Friday at 6:00pm. And the day of drop-off was Sunday at 6:00pm. I made sure that they knew when their weekends would start. I had been keeping track ever since the divorce hearing and made sure that they knew it. As I was about to explain how I felt about them being around her, Dogface said "I ask Drew all of the time why he never gets the kids. I just assumed that you didn't want them around me." I replied, "I didn't and I still don't. But he's just going to sneak and do it anyway so you need to know what I expect for my children."

She went on to say, "I got this apartment so that they can have a place to sleep. That's the only reason why I'm paying all of this rent, it's for them." I looked at her like she was crazy. She got an apartment for MY children? Clearly she didn't know that I'm the one that took Drew to get the application for the apartment a few weeks prior. And the only reason that I did it was because he told me that he was getting the apartment so that we could be together (Me, Drew and our children) in a safer neighborhood. Had I known that he was getting it to live with her, I wouldn't have taken him. He would have had his butt on the bus! Rather than saying this, I said "Well I don't know why you felt the need to do that because they have a home, and they have a mother and a father." In other words, you have no reason to even be in the picture. The look on her face said that she didn't like what I'd said but I didn't care. This crazy chick screwed and basically stole my husband. Does she really think that's she's going to steal my children too? When she started to respond, Pastor Kelly cut in again. He knew that it was about to get ugly. So he asked us how we were going to communicate as far as the children. Dogface spoke up again. This trick was getting way too comfortable. But that's when she said "I'll leave that up to them," pointing at Drew and I. Well how else did she think it was going to be? She wasn't standing in the middle of us when we said our vows. And she definitely wasn't there when we were making them so what else did she expect?

Again, Pastor Kelly asked about communication and how we would reach each other. Dogface spoke up again, "If she needs anything she can call my phone. We're (Drew and I) are always together anyway and we don't be doing anything." I looked at her like she was crazy. I turned and looked at Drew and said "You need to get a phone so that if I need to reach you, I can call you." Pastor Kelly agreed. I kept speaking, "And you also need to work on getting you your own place. You're a grown man and this is something that you need to do for you and your children." While I was speaking, Drew sat looking at me intently (with a dumb look on his face) and shaking his head like he understood, which is what he did during the entire meeting. I was shaking my head on the inside. I also brought up the idea of Drew picking up the children at a neutral location. I felt that it was a good idea since I didn't want him to come to my home. He agreed at the meeting, but he made it a point to say that he didn't want that at a later date.

The meeting went on for about another ten minutes. When Pastor Kelly told us that it was over, they got up and walked away. While Pastor Kelly and I were walking back to our cars, he stated, "Well we definitely see who's going to get things done. He's going to have a hard time getting away from her if he wants to leave her." In other words, Drew is not responsible enough to handle things and she's crazy. Well, those were my thoughts exactly.

Pretty much as soon as I got in my car, I started receiving texts from Drew. Dogface had this feature on her house phone where he could text me from it, even if he wasn't at her house. That's how he'd texted me. He texted me a bunch of stuff like, "So you don't love me no more? Are you serious? Is it really over? Are you seeing anyone? Why can't I pick the kids up at your house?" I didn't reply to any of these texts because I was driving. I was going to meet the kids; they were at their baseball practice. I drove by Drew and Dogface and they were in the car arguing. I really couldn't understand why all of this stuff that he was saying mattered. He had made his decision when he had walked out on our marriage. And I made sure to tell him this. Needless to say, he didn't stop bugging me. As a matter of fact, as soon as they had gotten to her mother's house, which is where they were driving to, he'd called me saying the same things. Would you believe that he actually started crying because I told him that we were over? Wait a minute. Is he seriously trying to make me feel guilty? I told him that the only reason we even had to have this meeting in the first place was because of his choices. And he had the nerve to disagree with me. When I tried to tell my mother how the meeting went, (she was at baseball practice), I kept being interrupted by Drew. And I showed her how many texts and calls I had received. I hate to say it, but the way that he was acting didn't stop there.

Chapter 16

Readjustment

The first time that Drew was supposed to come and get the kids, he was late getting them. I had to sing in the choir at a different church, Freedom Apostolic Church, and I didn't want to be late so I took the kids to my mother's house and made sure that Drew knew that he was supposed to pick them up there. This worked for me because I didn't want to see him and didn't want him at my house, anyway. As we agreed, he was supposed to get the kids at 6:00pm. I had to be at the church at 6:30pm so I had left my mom's at 6:00 pm. Clearly, when I had dropped the kids off at my mom's, he was already late. I was really irritated by this because Drew had known about the singing engagement in advance, and he also knows how I feel about being on time when I am going places.

I arrived at the church on time. By 7:00 pm, church still had not started, so I called my mom to see if Drew had shown up, which he had not. While we were waiting for the service to start, I was told that I was going to be leading a song that night. I was already uneasy about my children going with Drew and Dogface, so finding that out added much more pressure on me. On top of that, I had been sick with bronchitis and was just now beginning to recover. Around 8:00 pm, my mom called me to tell me that he had just gotten the kids and that he had Dogface in the car with him. Considering the situation, this was extremely disrespectful. It is bad enough that he does this to me, but to do this to my mother is unacceptable. My mother didn't like Dogface either and she didn't like that Drew had brought her to her house. She also didn't feel comfortable with my children going with them. So like me, she got out her blessed oil and prayed over the children. The difference between me and my mother is that I did it before he came into the house, so he didn't see me do it. Now, my mother, she did it right in front of them (Drew and Dogface). At a later time, he actually had the nerve to call me and tell me that it made him uncomfortable that she'd done that and that he felt like she was trying to be funny. Maybe she was, but there is no harm in prayer. I wasn't going to stop praying to make him feel comfortable in his mess and neither was my mother.

This particular night was really hard for me considering the circumstances, but it was life-changing. The spirit in the service was high, and God moved mightily. It was on that night that I learned to push past my pain and touch God in my worship when I minister in song. When I sang, it didn't matter that I did not feel well. It didn't matter that I was hurting on the inside. I learned to put my heart into my worship and when I did, God gave me strength. Elder Norman Williams, a speaker from Charlotte, North Carolina was the speaker for the evening. He took his text out of second Kings verse 5. Elder Williams spoke of Naaman and how he went to see the prophet to be healed of leprosy. It was on this night that I realized that God will put you in a dirty situation just to deliver you out of it. You cannot go to God with pride or disobedience in your heart and expect Him to move for you. When the prophet Elisha instructed Naaman to go down to the Jordan River and to dip himself in it seven times, Naaman didn't want to do it. He walked away angry feeling as though he'd made the long journey for nothing. The Jordan River was disgusting. Naaman actually had the nerve to say, "Couldn't Elisha at least come out to meet me? All that he had to do was touch me and call on the name of the Lord. And why couldn't he send me to any river other than one that is in Israel? At least the water would be cleaner." But when God deals with you, it's not always nice and clean. Sometimes the situations that God puts you in are downright filthy. You may not want to go through it, you may feel like giving up, and sometimes you may lose strength to the point where you cannot even walk and may have to crawl just to get out. But no matter how bad your situation is, God is a healer and a deliverer. You have to increase your faith and be obedient to the word of the Lord.

Naaman's servants asked him "Why didn't you do what the prophet said? If he said it, then it's going to come to pass." So when Naaman let go of his pride and believed, he went to the Jordan River, followed God's command and he was healed. When I walked out of church that night, I didn't leave the same way that I came. And I knew that my healing was on its way.

As Drew continued to get the kids on his weekends, his desire for control over me didn't diminish at all. I slowly began to release my anger and was "as sweet as pie" in my dealings with him. I do not know why he would even get the kids because he would text and be on the phone with me the entire weekend when he had them. By talking to Drew, I knew when the kids got up in the morning, what they ate and when they ate it, what they were doing, who was around them, and even what Drew was doing. He pretty much gave me a rundown of their whole weekend. But, what Drew was really trying to do was keep me talking to him so that I wouldn't have time to date or be around anyone else. Eventually, I learned to talk to him by text, and that was only it if was pertaining to the kids. The only time I spoke to him on the phone was when the kids wanted to talk to me and vice versa.

I did not like my children being around Drew in his current situation but eventually, I adjusted. I didn't hang out with a lot of people because I like to keep the drama in my life to a minimum. But since living like this was kind of lonely, I began to hang out with people every now and then. Shortly after, I found out that a guy from my church named Micah, had started his own business. He posted a status on Lookout that piqued my interest and I ended up going into business under him. Starting my own business was something that I needed because it gave me something to focus on other than my children. All mothers need an outlet, especially single mothers. We often get so lost in the identity and title of "mom" that we often forget that we are human beings that are very capable of doing other things too. As mothers, we often forsake our desires for the desires of our children. And sometimes it becomes so overwhelming that just the simple things, like wanting to have an "adult conversation" will make us happy. If we are not careful, getting lost in being a mother could lead to resentment and that is not an easy thing to bounce back from.

In order for the business to thrive, we had to have meetings, called PBR's, to recruit people and to have training amongst the group. I could only go to the trainings on the weekends that Drew had the children because any other time, I was without a babysitter. Saniyah's birthday came and I didn't really want to have a big party, so I had one at my house. Since we needed to have another meeting, I suggested that Micah come and introduce the business to the people that were at the party. I invited Tanya, our other business partner too. Micah introduced the business opportunity to the people that were there, but none were interested. He knew a lot of people that were there because most of them went to our church, so he hung around and had cake and ice cream along with everyone else.

Drew didn't show up to the party until it was almost over. When he did, he was uncomfortable. I fully believe that the only reason that he came was because it was his weekend to get the kids. This irritated me because I could not afford to have a party in the first place and the only reason that I did was because he kept pressing the issue. While he was there he stayed near me. He asked if I needed help, which by this time we were doing cake and ice cream and he saw that me and a few of the mothers at the party already had an assembly line going passing out plates. After all of the children from the party left, I went to get the kids bags ready so that they could go with Drew. It was raining really hard that night. Micah, Tanya, my mom and dad were still there, waiting for the rain to stop. While I was upstairs getting their bags ready, Drew came upstairs with me. While we were up there, he started asking me questions about Micah.

"Why is he here?"

"Didn't I tell you that he came to talk about the business? That's what he's here for." I was rude with my response because I asked him to come and support me with this business venture and he didn't.

"Is that the only reason he's here?"

"Huh?" I stopped what I was doing and looked at

him.

"Is he here for you too?"

"What difference does that make? You made your choice."

"No I didn't and I wish you would stop saying that. Is he here for you?"

But I didn't answer him. I continued getting the kids' things together. When I went back downstairs, Drew pulled his car close to the door so that he could get Saniyah's car seat and so that the children wouldn't get drenched by the rain when he took them to the car. After Drew and the children had left, my mom and dad left too. But Micah and Tanya were still there. We sat in the living room talking and watching The Word Network, a Christian channel on television. About five minutes after Drew had pulled off, he started calling and texting me to see what I was doing. He asked me again if Micah was there for me and if it was really over between me and him. I still couldn't understand why he would act like that considering the fact that he walked out of our marriage and was taking my children to the house that he shared with the woman that he left us for. Needless to say, I ignored all his calls. After a few calls, I told Micah and Tanya what Drew had asked me and showed them that he was calling. After I did, Micah said "I'm glad that you told me so now I at least know to watch my back. He might try to break my windows out of my car or beat me up or something." We laughed and talked a little more. But I started getting tired. I felt like it would be rude for me to ask them to leave so I waited until they were ready. My mom called me when she'd made it home, and to see if they were still there. After I told her yes, she said "The only reason Tanya is there is because of Micah." It was common knowledge in our church that Tanya had a tendency to be crazy. And we all knew that she liked Micah…a lot.

While we were talking, Micah decided to get up and

leave. He did this in the middle of our conversation. As soon as he stood up, Tanya stood up like she was getting ready to go too. I laughed in my head when I saw this because I knew that she was only there because he was there. What I did not know was WHY he was there. When Micah and I spoke to each other, it was always about business. We weren't cool enough for him to be at my house. I walked the both of them to the door. It was still raining really hard. Before Micah could walk out of the house, Tanya decided to take her keys out of her purse and hand them to Micah. When she tried to do this, he looked at her like she was crazy. She stood there for what seemed like five minutes with her arm stretched out and her keys still in her hand. Finally, Micah asked her "What are those for?"

She got an attitude with him and said "Stop playing. You know what they're for," with a look on her face that said "You better pull my car up." When she saw that Micah wasn't going to do it, she changed her attitude and tried to get that "sweet," (annoying to me) voice that women get with men when they want something, or when they think that they have some type of power over the man. "Will you pull my car up for me?" When she saw that he still wasn't going to do it, she said "please?" By this time I'm actually laughing out loud (I didn't mean to though). But Micah still didn't do it. So she stood there for a few more minutes looking at him. She took her glasses off, put them in her purse and walked to her car in the rain. She should have just done that in the first place. About thirty minutes after they had left, she called me to ask me if I thought that she was trying to "front" with the way that she acted with Micah. I told her that I felt like she did. She asked me why and I told her. Of course she didn't agree with me. But in talking to Micah later, he'd felt the same way, which is why he didn't move her car for her.

On a weekend that I had a PBR scheduled at my house I lost my car. It was a Thursday night around

11:00 pm when I heard a knock on the door. The knock terrified me because I was just now getting used to being in the house alone with the kids and my neighborhood wasn't the safest. I was still scared because someone had previously tried to break into my house. I was on the telephone with my mother when I walked to the door. When I looked out of the peephole, I saw a tow truck parked behind my car. Instantly, I was terrified. I had no idea what was about to happen. When I opened the door, there was a deputy sheriff standing there. He said that he was there to take my car because of a bill that I'd paid years ago; at least I thought that I had. He told me that in order to keep my car I would have to pay. I didn't even have a job and I was still on cash assistance so how in the world was I supposed to come up with the money? After they took my car, I couldn't stop crying. I called Drew to tell him what happened and he came right over. Of course he couldn't do anything to help because he didn't have any money either.

I tried everything that I could to get my car back. I had just spent about $1,000 in repairs on this car and you mean to tell me that I just wasted money that I was planning to use so that I could move out of town to spend on a car that was practically stolen? I did a consultation with different attorneys but couldn't afford to retain one. One attorney actually suggested that I just let them keep the car and get another one. Another suggested that I file bankruptcy in an effort to get in back. I couldn't afford to pay an attorney to do the bankruptcy for me. And I had no idea how to do it myself. I never got the money to get my car back and I was devastated. I had three children and no way to get where I needed to go. I didn't know how to catch the bus and had it just been me with no children, I would have learned. I felt that it was unfair to subject my children to standing in the cold for long periods of time waiting for public transportation. After I lost my car, Drew took the kids to school and took me to the grocery store or wherever I needed to go. That lasted for like a week and a half to two weeks. Even though I was still without transportation, I was kind of glad that he told me that he couldn't do it anymore because I was really uncomfortable riding in the car that he shared with Dogface. Her stuff was in the car, even her disgusting cigarette butts. The car was filthy and the entire situation pissed me off.

Shortly after this incident, Micah and I began to communicate more often. If I needed to go somewhere, he would take me, if I accepted his offer. When I did accept his offer, it was at times when my children weren't around because I didn't like to have men around my children, even though Micah and I were just friends. My children desperately wanted a father figure and a male in their lives and because of this they were easily attached to people and I didn't want them to be confused. Communication between Micah and I started out because of the business but through this situation and over time, I learned that we had a lot in common and we became friends. Over time, we became much more.

Chapter 17

One Last Time

Drew continued to get the kids for the next month. By the time that November came around, this stopped. November 2, 2013 was the last time that he came to get them for his weekend and he was almost four hours late. Even though he would not find the time to get his children, he found the time to have sex when I called him. I'm sorry to admit that I had had a weak moment and had failed again. It was near Thanksgiving and I was really emotional. I missed spending the holidays with my husband and my children. Needless to say, having sex with Drew didn't restore our marriage. In fact, it did nothing but make me feel worse than I had before I did it. Of course Drew promised that he would spend the holidays with us, but he didn't. Shortly after, I found out that Dogface, the woman that he'd left us for was pregnant, again. My friend Chelsea had called to tell me that she had seen it on Dogface's Lookout page. She didn't know how to approach the subject but felt that she had to inform me because she knew that he was still trying to come back to me.

The boys' sixth birthday was coming up. I knew that they were still missing their dad so I did what most parents do when the other parent is missing; I tried to over-compensate them for not having a father around. Now, I am not saying that I was right in doing so, but I did it anyway. On the day of the boy's birthday, I took cookies and balloons to their school so that they could have a party there. Drew told me that he was coming to help but he didn't, and I had made sure that he knew the time the teacher had asked us to come.

I had asked the boys what they wanted to do for their birthday. They told me that they wanted to go to dinner so I planned to do it on the weekend. I made sure that they understood that we weren't going out on their birthday and asked them what they wanted me to cook for them. I remember making them everything that they requested, even though it didn't make any sense to me. And then they had the nerve to be ungrateful. I was so upset. On top of exhausting myself in the kitchen, I was upset because after we had left the school, Drew had called and apologized for not showing up and said that he would come and spend time with them that evening. Well, he didn't. When the weekend arrived, he didn't show up to their birthday dinner either. But for the first time ever, his mother came. Out of all of the birthday parties, baby showers and events we had, this was the first ever that she had come to. She felt out of place though, out of embarrassment of her son and the things that he'd done to me and our children. I've told her time and time again that she can't control what he does and that the choices that he made are not her fault. But she still feels otherwise.

Christmas had come and gone and Drew didn't come to see the kids. They had asked him to come and spend time with them and that's all that they wanted from him for Christmas. As a Christmas gift, Drew's mom had bought the kids a dresser for their bedroom. Drew showed up 3 days after Christmas at about 11:00 pm with the dresser and some gifts for the kids. He had gotten 3 pairs of pajamas for each of the kids. It's a shame when it's a surprise that the father of your children actually buys something for them. But I simply told him "thank you." To me, this was nothing to get excited about because he didn't have a job, so most likely Dogface had bought them. I'd gotten to the point where my mindset had changed from "You need to help me take care of these kids," to "I do everything for my children and anything you do is just a bonus." It may seem a little harsh, but in my case I think of it as "survival."

Without even realizing it, I was really bitter and upset about the way that my life had turned out. The things that I had gone through had caused damage to my self-esteem and self-worth. And in turn, it had ruined so many of my relationships. People that I had talked to regularly began to fade in the distance. Being unhappy was becoming very draining for me. I knew within myself that this was not how I wanted to live. And I did not want to feel this way anymore. So, I made up my mind that I was going to do whatever I could to change my life. I went to church on New Year's Eve with the full intent to not leave the same way that I came. I'd had a strong desire to be free for years. But I knew that my deliverance was near and I was ready for it.

The New Year's Eve service was awesome. It was

during this service that I released all of the pain that I had endured over the last seven plus years. I released all of the hurt from the abuse and abandonment of my ex-husband. On that night, I released Drew. I honestly walked out free and my spirit felt much lighter. How did I know that I was truly free? I knew because the devil came right away to test me.

The day after New Year's Day, I returned back to the place where I was volunteering. While I was there, I received a phone call from Drew's cousin, Talisa. Apparently, he had called her telling her that he missed his family and that he wanted to come home to me and his children. Again, this was news to me because I hadn't even spoken to Drew and hadn't heard anything of the sort. When I told her this, she was confused. She didn't know that he hadn't even come to me to talk to me about it. This really disturbed me because he's a grown man and we had been married for god's sake. He couldn't come and talk to me himself? Why would he send someone to talk to me for him?

After discussing this, I informed her that I wasn't interested. I told her that he had a baby on the way with Dogface and that this sudden "change of heart" probably had something to do with that. While we were on the telephone, she went on Lookout to confirm that Dogface was pregnant. Dogface had put a picture of an ultrasound on her page. I told her to tell him that if he wants to come home, then he needs to come to me himself. I was just going to tell him no, but it was the principle of the whole thing.

Even though I knew that I didn't want to be with Drew, a seed had been planted in my mind and a few weeks later, it began to grow. I began to miss him periodically and wonder if I could really go on living the rest of my life without him. I began to wonder if I could really raise three children alone. I knew without a shadow of a doubt that I didn't want to. But what were my options? What man will want me with three children?

What if God never sends anyone? Will my children grow up without a father AND without a father figure? Will I have to settle for less just to have someone? Will I have to reduce my standards and expectations?

Going through a divorce and all of the other things that I'd gone through placed these doubts and insecurities in my mind and they were hard to overcome. But I can stand here and tell you that with the grace of God, you can overcome any doubts, insecurities, shortcomings, and failures that you may be experiencing. You can overcome anything "because greater is He that is in you, than He that is in the world" (1 John 4:4 KJV). You don't have a reason to doubt yourself because you are "fearfully and wonderfully made" (Psalm 139:14). I knew that I shouldn't have had these types of thoughts so I began to pray because I wanted to be transformed in my mind. I wanted to think differently. As I began to pray, God spoke peace to my soul. As I began to think on Him, I felt better. It became easier to live another day and I began to become "content" in my current situation.

Even in my state of contentment, I don't know why, but I decided to have one last conversation with Drew to see where we stood. It was the month of February when he had come to my house so that we could talk. After the incident with his cousin, he had come to me himself and told me that he wanted to come home. When Drew arrived at my house the day that we had the conversation, I asked him if what he had said to me was true and he confirmed it. When I asked how he expected this to work, he said that he didn't know. For clarification, I asked again if he was sure that he wanted to be home with me and his children and he said yes, so I asked him how bad he wanted it and what he would do to prove it. After listening to Drew express how he would do anything to have his family back, I threw out a suggestion to see if he was serious. I told him that I had heard that he had a baby on the way and asked if it were true. Now, anyone that knows Drew knows that he is a liar and will lie about any and everything no matter how big or small. But Drew actually confessed that he had gotten Dogface pregnant. Of course he was scared to. But if I were in his position, I would want to deny it too, simply out of humiliation.

After Drew's confession, I made a suggestion. I told him that I understood that he had a baby on the way and that it was not a problem for me. The problem was not the baby, but was the baby's mother. I told him that I loved him but I refuse to deal with Dogface for the rest of my life. This girl has been a problem in our ENTIRE relationship and I'd made it to the point in my life where I decided that I would have peace, whether he was in my life or not. After making sure that Drew understood what I was saying, I went on with my suggestion. I told him that if he wanted to make our marriage work, then he would either have to sign over his rights to the baby and not deal with Dogface or the baby at all, or have her sign over her rights and we raise the baby, along with our three children together. The look on his face when I said this was a look of total shock. His reaction was as though I had punched him in his stomach and he had lost his wind for a few minutes. Drew asked me, "You would actually do that?" Yes, I would have done that. But I was beyond tired of Dogface and her drama. And anyone that knows her knows that drama is all that she is made of. I wouldn't put myself or my children in a position to where we would have to live a life similar to that of a roller coaster ride ever again. After expressing that to him, I told him that my only concern as far as taking the baby was whether it was going to be mentally ill or not. It is hard raising three children alone, two of which are extremely hyperactive. So although it may seem unfair, I did not want to add a child to the mix that may have mental problems. After finishing the conversation with Drew, he asked if he could have a few days to think about it. I told him yes. He never brought the subject up to me again, and neither did I.

Now, Drew has a baby with Dogface. I saw her about a month or so after she had had the baby while I was at the salon that she and I go to get our eyebrows waxed. And this girl was actually trying to hold a conversation with me like we were friends. I forgave her, but that does not change the fact that I do not like her. Even if she had never taken a part in destroying my marriage, I wouldn't have ever liked her simply because I have this thing where I like to keep the drama in my life to a minimum. And, I just don't deal with crazy people. Although I was upset with her for talking about me and my children to the lady that does our eyebrows and acting as though she had nothing to do with the demise of our marriage, I let it go and moved on with my life. I wish her, and her baby happiness. She's going to need all of the happiness and blessings that she can get because the bible clearly states, "Be not deceived; God is not mocked: for whatsoever a man soweth, that shall he also reap" (Galatians 6:7 KJV). Not only that, but she has a baby with a man that left his pregnant wife and two children. He does not take care of or have a relationship with the three children that he has with me. It will be a hard lesson for her to learn that he's going to do her, and her baby the same way.

It didn't take long for Dogface to learn. Drew did her the same way that he did me. Come to find out, he left her when she was pregnant to be with another woman, a woman whom he eventually married. Nevertheless, God is not mocked. And He will get the glory, even out of this situation.

Post-Logue

Finally Free

I became free and totally delivered after finally finishing a book by T.D. Jakes called "Let it Go: Forgive So You Can Be Forgiven." I knew that most of my problems came from harboring bitterness and unforgiveness in my heart. What I did not know was how to forgive my ex-husband. A part of me felt like by forgiving him and letting the situation go, I was giving up on him and that I never really loved him. By reading the book on forgiveness, I found that just because our marriage died, it did not mean that we never loved each other. It also didn't mean that the love that I had for him expired along with our marriage. In the book, T.D. Jakes gave an example of losing a loved one to death. He reminded us that when the person died, the love that we had for the person wasn't buried with them and the fact that they passed on didn't make us love the person any less. In fact, we can still very much love someone, even while they are in the grave.

As I began to finish the book, I took notes and made a journal of everything that spoke directly to me and my situation. Continuing my reading, I found that the unforgiveness in my heart was like a poison and as I prayed and continued to read, I could literally feel the poison of unforgiveness being drawn out of my body likened to the treatment that a dialysis patient receives. During a dialysis treatment, the doctor uses a machine that pulls out all of the contaminated blood, purifies it and then inputs it back into the body. This is exactly what

God did for me. After being cleansed, God made me whole. And walking in the "newness of life," (Romans 6:1-4) I felt like a brand new person.

Not realizing it at the time, after becoming free I found myself walking right back into the same type of bondage that God had delivered me from. Although my spiritual discernment was sharp, I allowed myself to be manipulated once again, and my eyes to be covered with "rose-colored glasses." Even though I was content in the current state that I was in, I am human and I still had a strong desire to be married and for my children to have a father. The friendship that I mentioned previously with Micah had begun to grow and a strong bond was built upon mutual experiences, beliefs, characteristics and desires. Many people have told me, "he's not even cute," but he unbeknownst to them, he had a personality and charisma that would allure you and pull on you. I became spell-bound.

Before I knew it, I had sacrificed two and a half

years of my life, sacrificed my body, my anointing and my peace on a person that made a commitment to me and snatched it back. I was so gone, mentally; that I did not even realize how much time had gone by until I began to feel God tugging on my spirit. It was then that I realized that I was bound...once again. Once again, I began to pray for deliverance and every time I had a breakthrough, I found myself right back in sin with him. It became a game of tug-of-war. I was at war between my spirit and my flesh, heaven and hell, life and death. The game played for so long that I lost track of time. Yet again, my deliverance came through an enormous amount of pain. The person that I loved began to cheat on me and eventually left me for the person that used to be my best friend, Ashanti...and although Micah and my relationship was not known to everyone, I felt that she knew that Micah and I were together.

Again, I found myself harboring bitterness and resentment, and wanting to seek revenge. Once more,

I had to be reminded of the scripture that says "Be not deceived; God is not mocked: for whatsoever a man soweth, that shall he also reap" (Galatians 6:7 KJV). Not only will they reap what they have sown, I had to reap too. I reaped for walking in disobedience. Even in my disobedience, I learned that God still loves me. He was faithful to me when I wasn't faithful to Him. After much prayer, I received my deliverance again.

When I look back over my life and think of the many things that God has done for me, the only two words that come to mind are "Thank You." Thank You Jesus for setting me free. He saw me while I was wandering, lost on a path of self-destruction. In my worse times, He spoke peace to my soul and assured me that I was not alone. He was a comforter in the midnight hour. When I felt alone, He held my hand. His word gave me guidance and it paved a path for me to follow. When I felt like I couldn't go on, He gave me strength. When I had nearly lost my mind, He restored it for me. Each time that I began to feel my mind slip, He brought it back. And a scripture would come to mind, "Thou wilt keep him in perfect peace, whose mind is stayed on thee: because he trusteth in thee" (Isaiah 26:3). Each day as I began to think on Him, each moment felt a little bit lighter. As the hours began to pass, it became easier and the days began to shine brighter.

Plenty of times I felt like I couldn't make it through the day. During these times, I would pray and ask God to give me strength just to make it through the day, not through the next week, but through the day. My heart would ache so bad that I felt like the pain that I was feeling was suffocating me. The pain was so severe that I couldn't breathe. After praying to God for strength, strength would instantly come into my body and at a loss for words, all that I could squeeze out was "Thank You." Although I trusted in God and I believed His word, never before had I prayed a prayer and received instantaneous results. This assured me that the God that

I serve is real. And as I learned to put my total trust in Him, I began to feel free, and I could breathe again.

As I began to get to know Him better, He would reveal Himself to me in His Word. I began to dream dreams, and see visions. He would give me warnings of things that were about to take place and a few moments after envisioning it, it would happen. Sometimes it would frighten me because He would show me things that I didn't want to know. But I still trusted Him and believed that everything would "work out for me because I loved Him" (Romans 8:28) and because He cares for me. "Casting all your care upon him; for he careth for you" (1 Peter 5:7).

Over time, God became everything to me and as He was faithful to me, I was faithful to Him. He stood in the gap of every empty area in my life. He filled the void of losing my husband and closest friend. He was there when I had no one that I could turn to. When I couldn't provide for my children, He provided for me. When I couldn't sleep, He gave me "sweet rest." God healed me and His love changed my life.

I had spent years trying to become free of the bondage that I was trapped in. I was stuck on this even path, "in neutral," and I was all alone. I had lost all of my friends. I felt like my family had disowned me. All that I had left was my children, and I was so empty that I didn't have anything to give them. The test that I was stuck in was very painful. I would liken it to death because the person that I once was; was dead. I no longer knew who I was. I had let this person destroy my confidence, my faith, my integrity and ultimately, my life. I know now that where I was trapped, was a journey to a greater anointing, to greater power, and greater strength. While trapped in this journey, I learned my purpose for living. I did not go through this because God is a cruel God. I suffered so that God could prove Himself to me. And the same God that delivered me out of bondage is the same God that can deliver you. My testimony will help someone else to know that they too can be set free. I urge you today to walk in the liberty that God has granted you. "If the Son therefore shall make you free, ye shall be free indeed" (John 8:36 KJV). And I no longer NEED to be free. I AM FREE.

www.ingramcontent.com/pod-product-compliance
Lightning Source LLC
Chambersburg PA
CBHW031413290426
44110CB00011B/363